THE FACTS AND THE FICTION

STOCK MARKET RULES

50 of the
Most Widely Held
Investment Axioms
Explained, Examined
and Exposed

MICHAEL D. SHEIMO

PROBUS PUBLISHING COMPANY
Chicago, Illinois
Cambridge, England

This publication is designed to provide accurate and authoritative information in regard to the subject matter covered. It is sold with the understanding that the author and the publisher are not engaged in rendering legal, accounting, or other professional service.

Authorization to photocopy items for internal or personal use, or the internal or personal use of specific clients, is granted by PROBUS PUBLISHING COMPANY, provided that the U.S. $7.00 per page fee is paid directly to Copyright Clearance Center, 222 Rosewood Drive, Danvers, MA 01923, USA; Phone: 1-508-750-8400. For those organizations that have been granted a photocopy license by CCC, a separate system of payment has been arranged. The fee code for users of the Transactional Reporting Service is 1-55738-525-4/94/$00.00 + $7.00.

ISBN 1-55738-525-4

Printed in the United States of America

IPC

1 2 3 4 5 6 7 8 9 0

DEDICATION

To my partner,
best friend
and inspiration,
my wife Linda

Contents

Preface

In the past two hundred years plus, the stock market has developed a great number of axioms, sayings which relate directly to the timing or strategies of buying and selling stocks. Most of these axioms have inspiration and wisdom behind them. The stock trader who truly understands the implications of the sayings has great advantages in the stock market. The sayings can provide helpful strategies, particularly during difficult times.

Many of these "well worn" sayings change from time to time and are credited to new authors. The modern "Never fight the fed" (Chapter 25) is similar to a statement from the early 1900's ". . . it depends on government action." "Cut your losses and let your profits soar" has now changed to "sell the losers and let the winners run." The words have changed, but the meaning stays the same.

Knowledge of the axiom alone is not enough. It is essential to understand the meaning behind the saying. Axioms can bring up any number of questions. If it is better to "sell the losers and let the winners run," (Chapter 1) how does one determine which stock is a winner? Is price alone the only deliberation or are there other factors to consider? If the investor continually sells the losers, how and when does profit-taking become an event? Answers to questions such as these can give the investor a strong understanding of the full meaning behind the axiom.

"Averaging Up," in a stock position might be better than "averaging down," but why is it better? When is it better and how can it be done? (Chapter 4)

If money is continually lost on "stop loss" orders what can be done to correct the situation? Are there better times or better ways to make use of stop orders? What strategy can be used if the investor wants to buy a stock only when the price begins a significant move in an upward direction? (Chapter 17)

When a stock is heavily owned by institutions is it a disadvantage or an advantage? What special precautions can be taken or different tactics considered? (Chapter 18)

These are just a few of the basic concepts covered by the book. A review of the Chapter Headings offers the investor a quick reference guide to more than fifty different market situations.

Throughout the book there are charts shown and points made about stocks of several different corporations. The information should not necessarily be taken as current buy or sell or hold recommendations. The data merely presents clear examples for specific situations.

The major difficulties encountered by the individual investor are hesitation and understanding. Hesitation can be costly, it can result in lost dollars or lost opportunities. Anything the individual investor can do to decrease the time lost to indecision will improve the chances for more profitable trades. A basic understanding of some of the finer points of buying and selling stocks can be an even larger concern. Placing a buy or sell order on a stock is not difficult. In fact, it is almost too easy. The difficulty arises in knowing when, how and what kind of order to place. This is where Stock Market Rules will be of assistance.

The "rules" discussed in this book are axioms based on ideas for trading stocks. These concepts are explained, examined and exposed, in order to bring an understanding of some of the finer points of stock trading to the individual. An understanding of these concepts will improve the decision-making process and enhance the timing of buying and selling stocks. This improvement can quickly lead to higher profits and bring greater enjoyment to investing in the stock market.

Chapter 1
Sell the Losers and Let the Winners Run

The title of this chapter is one of the oldest sayings in the stock market. In the late 1800s, Daniel Drew had a slightly different version of it:

"Cut your losses and let your profits run."

The concept is sound. It is prudent for an investor to sell stocks that are losing money and could continue to drop in price and value. It makes equally good sense to stay with stocks showing significant gains as long as they remain fundamentally strong.

But just what is a loser? Is it any price drop from the high? Is a stock a loser only if the investor is actually in a loss position? That being a current price below the investor's original purchase price.

Any price drop is a losing situation; these are stocks currently costing the investor money. They are a loss of profits. In some situations the investor should prepare to sell, but in other circumstances it is time for a closer look before reaching the sell decision.

The determination of whether a stock is still a winner depends on the cause of a price correction. If the cause of a price drop appears to be a weakness in the overall market situation or the "normal" daily fluctuation of the stock price, it can still be a winner.

If the cause has more long-term implications it can be time to take the loss and move on. Some long-term implications are:

- Lower sales being reported
- New tax difficulties being encountered
- New legal problems
- The recent emergence of a bear market
- Any other costly situations which impact earnings

Any situation that has a negative impact on the longer term picture of earnings or earnings growth can quickly turn a stock into a loser. Many investors will sell at this point to cut the loss and move on to potential winner.

Value, in terms of growth potential, is based on earnings and earnings growth. The investor must observe the stock in action and make a judgement decision as to whether the value of a stock is more likely to increase, remain flat or begin to decline.

This can be difficult at times since a winner can temporarily take on the appearance of a loser.

There are three situations which can make a winner look weak, but are not necessarily a signal to begin selling. These are temporary situations and that makes them exceptions to the rule.

Exception 1. Stock prices fluctuate up or down in day-to-day trading. A glance at any daily price chart will easily show what may be considered normal daily fluctuation for any individual stock. Stocks also move from one trading range to another. For example, a stock could have a daily fluctuation of 30 dollars to 35 dollars, but would occasionally move to 40 dollars, then could drop back to the 30 to 35 dollar fluctuation. The trading range would be considered 30 to 40. When the stock moves up and begins fluctuating between 40 to 55, it is considered to be trading in a new and higher range.

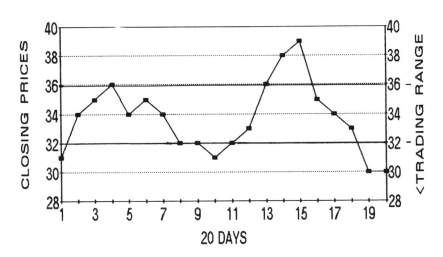

DAILY TRADING RANGE
PRICE IN DOLLARS

20 DAYS

This is a bit of an oversimplification as it would be unusual to find a stock that fluctuates in exact one dollar amounts, but it does illustrate daily fluctuation and trading range. Both the trading range movement and the daily fluctuations can be readily observed on a price pattern chart. The investor should take the time to become familiar with the trading ranges and fluctuations from the past few months. This familiarity will illustrate what can be considered a "normal" fluctuation and what might be a breakout or breakdown to a new trading range. If a lower stock price is within the normal range it can still be considered a winner, even if the investor is experiencing a small loss. This is assuming that the initial analysis has shown the stock to be a winner in earnings and growth. Therefore, this kind of weakness is probably not the time to sell out and take a loss.

Exception 2. A significant drop in the overall stock market can force the price of any winner to lower levels. All stocks can eventually become losers. In most cases this is a time for concern, but not necessarily panic. As we have seen in recent years, the stock market can drop 100 to 200 points and recover rather quickly. Usually, stocks that were winners before the correction will most likely be winners when the market regains its stability and recovers.

If the market drop appears to continue, the investor should seriously consider selling and moving to the sideline. September of 1987 (October was too late) would have been excellent timing for this strategy. If the market correction is sudden and appears to stabilize in just a few days, it can be best to hold the position and even consider buying more shares of the same stock. This could have been an effective strategy in the 1989 October correction.

Market drops or corrections do not necessarily turn winning stocks into losers, unless they are severe and extended over a few weeks and months. The extended market drops are bear markets, which tend to turn most stocks into losers.

Exception 3. A significant upward move to a new trading range, followed by some price weakness is a fairly normal occurrence. As a stock makes a major upward movement, many investors will begin to take profits. There is certainly nothing wrong with taking profits, but the stock might not be near the end of its climb. In fact, the true advance in price might only have just started. Even so, it is inevitable that some profit taking will occur and the stock that has risen to new highs will show some downward correction in price. Again, this doesn't necessarily make the stock a loser.

A loser stock is one which is dropping and will probably go lower in price. There are stronger reasons for the stock to drop than for it to rise. The reasoning is virtually always based on lower earnings or earnings growth.

A signal can be observed if a stock begins to fall lower than its usual daily trading range and the overall market is unchanged or advancing. If a stock that usually trades between

45 to 50 dollars a share drops to 43 and then to 40, it is time to be concerned. This is especially true if similar stocks and the broad markets are advancing. It becomes important to either find out why the decline is taking place or sell the stock and cut the losses.

Winners are stocks showing consistent growth in income and earnings, as well as development into new or existing markets with innovative products. The main line products of consistent winners are products that have an increasing market. They are not passing fads. Even though a product may have created a tremendous desire demand, how likely is this demand going to remain strong in the next three to five years? Pet rocks and cabbage dolls can have a strong market impact for a year or two, but seldom are able to build enduring demand over the years. Faddish products can be excellent earnings boosters for well-established companies, but are usually not on a firm enough foundation on which to build an entire company.

Although winner stocks can experience occasional difficulties, they tend to have strong five-year earnings growth and are currently continuing to nearly match or exceed that growth at the current time. If a company is showing a 20 percent annual earnings growth rate for the past five years and is currently showing similar growth, it is a potential winner. This stock can be especially attractive if the periodic price weaknesses coincide with overall market drops. As long as the earnings and growth are maintained or increased and the stock price continues to rise, it is a winner and will likely remain a winner.

Winners should be held until the fundamentals which make them winners begin to weaken or until the price runs too far ahead of the earnings, which causes a decline in value. If the growth of earnings does not keep pace with the advancing price, the stock could easily turn into a loser.

Losers that are taking money from the investor should be sold and forgotten until they stabilize and begin to build the fundamental strength necessary to become winners.

Chapter 2

Make Winners Win Big

It was Jessie Livermore who indicated the importance of winning big when the investor's conclusions, based on analysis, are correct. Being right only half of the time is usually enough if, when you win, you win big.

Winning stocks are a special situation. Difficult though it might be, it is important to establish a price objective, also called a sell target, at which the stock will be sold for a profit.

Price Objective

When the price of a stock, which is now at 30 dollars a share, reaches 40 dollars it will be sold. This price objective should be adhered to and the stock sold, unless an unusual situation warrants an increase in the target price.

The only event which will make a stock price rise is the presence of more buyers than sellers. Buyers are attracted because they believe the price of the stock will rise higher. They might be attracted to the value of the stock or they could be attracted to an even higher anticipated value (sometimes referred to as perceived value). There are three situations that tend to bring buyers to the market and make a stock rise in price:

- Increase in earnings or earnings anticipation.
- General market move.

- Takeover rumor / manipulation.[1]

If any of these conditions occur and a stock does not rise in price, there could be something wrong with the actual value or the perceived value. If the problem with the price of the stock is in the perceived value this can be called an "undervalued" situation and a potentially good investment.

Improved earnings are generally caused by:

- New large contracts
- Lowered interest rates
- Winning a legal judgment
- Lending confidence inspired by a strong bull market.

These are all sound reasons for the stock price to rise and therefore to increase the price objective target.

The emergence of a buy-out offer can be another good reason to carefully raise the price objective. In fact, these positive influences on the price of the stock can become a reason to actually buy more shares and increase the size of the stock position. Raising a price objective can be particularly effective in a bull market, where the upward price movement of an individual stock is increased by the momentum of the general market trend.

The raising of a price objective in a flat or bearish market should be done with a great deal of caution. The market can pull the individual stock price down during a bearish move as the prices of all stocks drop lower.

Few investors or advisors would debate the strategy of letting the winners run. The winner is the stock everyone

---

1   Manipulation is included with takeover rumor as the two tend to go together, although it is certainly possible to have manipulation without a takeover rumor.

wants to buy, the stock that is increasing in price. It's common sense to let an advancing stock keep running up in price. The money invested is doing what it is supposed to be doing; the action of the price of the stock is in line with the strategy. As long as the earnings of the stock and the market remain strong, there is no good reason to sell the stock. If enough cash is available, the investor should consider "averaging up"[2] with additional purchases of the same winning stock. Buying additional shares of the same stock will allow the investor to "build a position." This is the way to win big with a profitable stock.

Averaging Up

In the example below, there are five purchases of stocks. Each purchase is for 100 shares of the same stock. The per share price for each transaction increases with each purchase (because the stock price is rising), but the cumulative average price per share is actually lowered. The same quantity of the same stock is purchased with each buy transaction.

1. Buy 100 Shares at $30.00 Each:
   Average Cost: $30.00
   Total Shares Owned: 100

2. Buy 100 Shares at $35.00 Each:
   Average Cost: $32.50
   Total Shares Owned: 200

3. Buy 100 Shares at $40.00 Each:
   Average Cost: $35.00
   Total Shares Owned: 300

4. Buy 100 Shares At $45.00 Each:
   Average Cost: $37.50
   Total Shares Owned: 400

2　*See* Chapter 4.

5.   Buy 100 Shares At $50.00 Each
     Average Cost: $40.00
     Total Shares Owned: 500

     Average Cost Per Share = $40.00
     ($20,000 divided by 500 shares.)

     Average Profit Per Share = $10.00
     (current price per share $50.00,
       less the average cost of $40.00)

Each share of the last group of 100 shares had a 10 dollar profit built in at the time of purchase. Buying a stock with profit built into the purchase is an enviable position: as the price continues to advance and the investor continues to make purchases, the per share cost is lowered and the potential profit increases. This is a strategy frequently used by institutional investors and investment advisors. It requires a bit more planning and calculation, but it is sound investment practice.

It is also appropriate to consider protective "sell stop" orders (when possible) on the stock that has been running up in price. This will protect the profits of the earlier purchased stock and will limit possible losses on the shares purchased later.[3]

So when does one sell and take the profits? The question is difficult, even for professionals. The time to sell for profits can be determined by any one of the following conditions.

Price Objective. The attainment of a price objective, which is based on the value comparison between the current price and current earnings growth (not necessarily the PE ratio), can determine a sell. If a stock has experienced an annual growth rate of 20 percent over the last five years and that

---

3   *See* Chapter 17.

rate has now slipped to 15 or 10 percent, the value of the stock is declining.

If the price is continuing to increase and the earnings remain the same, the inherent value of the stock is actually declining. If the earnings are increasing with the price of the stock, then this inherent value is also increasing. It is also important to keep in mind that "perceived value" (as determined by heavy buying of the stock) can be a more important factor than actual value. This usually means that many investors believe the future earnings will improve significantly.

Stopped Out. Being "stopped out" is having a stop order executed.[4] This is the time to look at alternative stocks that fit the investment objectives. However, if the price of the stopped out stock keeps dropping low enough it is possible to consider repurchasing the same stock.

Better Opportunity. Finding a better growth opportunity can be a valid reason to sell a stock. Selecting a new stock can be a difficult decision to make; it also takes time to research. New growth opportunities should be selected in advance and should have somewhat similar characteristics to the stock recently sold. The investment theme or play can change, but the value basics of selection should be similar.

Letting the winners run is a good basic concept, but it is possible to let the price run until it drops. Eventually the price of the stock will begin to out-pace earnings growth and, therefore, value. If the stock continues to rise, the price increase is based on earnings anticipation. This can occur when the profit taking begins, and can be followed by a decline in price. Although the turning point can be difficult to anticipate, it can be defined as the ideal price at which profits should be taken and reinvested in another growth stock.

---

4   *See* Chapter 16.

Chapter 3

Losers Demand Careful Strategy

The strategy for underperforming stocks can be as important as the strategy for winners. Sometimes this is not as simple as selling the stock. The strategy takes time to research and plan whether to buy more stock, hold the position or sell. Also, there is the selection of a new stock to buy, once the losing stock is sold. Ideally, most of this research has been done before a problem arises.

Situations can arise where it is too late to take a loss in a particular stock: the damage has been done, and to sell out would not yield significant dollars (because the price of the stock has dropped too low). There will not be enough money left to invest in another stock.

It is also possible to have a stock beset by selling that is still a good stock. Its actual value (determined by earnings) might have increased, even though the market price has declined. In fact, it could become a candidate for further investment. These situations call for specific strategies rather than a general approach.

Selling Out and Repositioning

If stocks are turning into losers, a great deal of time can be required for their recovery. Time is important as it means lost profit potential. The stock can be sold and the assets can be allocated elsewhere, thereby making up the loss and bringing new gains.

When a decision is made to sell a stock it should be sold as immediately as possible. This can be crucial timing. The stock should usually be sold at the "market" price. Placing a limit sell order can cause delays and possible loss of profits (because it might not be possible to have a limit order executed). Time and timing become more important than trying to squeeze out an extra eighth or quarter of a dollar.

Likewise the new stock should be purchased immediately. Here are some important considerations before selling the stock.

- Can the assets be better allocated (invested elsewhere)? This might not be possible in a down market. The obvious plan would be to select new stocks for investment on a continual basis. Many investors will decide which stock to buy next, before they decide on which stock will be sold.

- Selling underperforming stocks in a bull market makes sense. If other investors liked the stock, it would not be underperforming. It should not be difficult to find better stocks.

- In a flat to bearish market, the investor might consider other alternatives, such as placing the funds in a temporary investment, perhaps a money market fund.

- If one is to take a loss, it can be worthwhile to follow the "no more than 10 to 15 percent loss" strategy. This is taking a loss sooner rather than later. If a loss is already greater than 10 to 15 percent, alternative strategies could be in order. Taking a loss is somewhat easier if there are also offsetting gains from other, profitable sells.

Once the strategy has been planned, it should be implemented as immediately as possible.

Situations can arise where selling might not be the preferable strategy. It can be advantageous to take a larger position in the stock by buying more shares.

Taking An Investment Position

Another side to the strategy for underperforming stocks would be to take "an investment position" in the losing stock. This refers to a practice of lowering the cost basis of the investment by buying at reduced prices. Although the wisdom of this strategy is debated, it can be a valid strategy in some situations.

An investment position can be used with a stock that has had a recent setback caused by temporary conditions, such as a weakening in earnings growth just as the market experiences a severe correction. The price drop can occur before an individual has the opportunity to sell out and take a reasonable loss.

For example, in 1986, Dayton Hudson, a mid-western department store, announced weak earnings for the early part of the year. The stock dropped from the high 58 dollar range down to the low 40s. The following year, in 1987, Dayton Hudson began climbing toward former levels. Takeover rumors began to appear. The stock ran up as high as 63 dollars a share. The only problem was the timing; October of 1987, was swiftly approaching.

After the October "correction," Dayton Hudson stock plummeted to 21 1/2 dollars a share. Earnings remained relatively strong in this time period and increased significantly in 1988 and 1989.

Earnings per share

1986	1987	1988	1989
$2.62	$2.41	$3.45	$4.25
	(8%)	+43%	+23%

Sales per share

1986	1987	1988	1989
$95.09	$124.48	$157.17	$175.90
	+30%	+26%	+12%

It is easy to see that sales remained strong, even though the earnings and price were showing weakness in 1987. From the low price of 21 1/2 dollars a share, after the market setback in 1987, Dayton Hudson stock began a steady climb to above the sixty dollar mark in the summer of 1989.

Taking an investment position has its risk, but can be a strategy for turning a loss into a profit. The strategy is best used with companies which have been around for many years and have some diversification of product line. These companies tend to be more stable and have the capabilities to weather financial difficulties and market swings.

The investor should have some fundamental reasons for believing that the company earnings will recover, remain stable or continue to grow. Asking questions such as these can help the investor make the decision to take an investment position:

- Why is the stock currently losing?
- Has the stock recovered from former difficult times?
- What are three good reasons to keep the stock and/or add to the position?
- How much time will be spent waiting for the recovery?

The decision to sell is made much less complicated by the analysis necessarily involved in taking an investment position. In many cases, selling and taking the loss is the best course of action, but it can be useful to be aware of these alternative courses of action.

Holding For Recovery

Another alternative is to simply hold the stock and wait for the price to recover. It could take some time, but if the initial investment is of a reasonable size, the drop is sudden and severe and the investor does not have the funds available to average down, holding might be the way to go.

Holding might be most appropriate if most of the damage has already occurred and the value of the stock has significantly declined. If an individual has invested ten thousand dollars in a stock, which is now worth less than a thousand dollars, there isn't much that can be done with the limited remaining dollars. There isn't enough money to take another reasonable stock position. Although this is a loss, the investor is still holding shares that have a potential for recovery. If the investor decides to hold, the condition of the market is usually irrelevant. It is an individual stock decision, not a market decision.

A word of caution on the hold strategy. Some companies will decline in price due to bad earnings only to be bought out by another company who sees the price as a bargain. This can create an unwanted loss for the investor. If the Dayton Hudson Company had been bought out by some other company, at 40 or even 50 dollars a share, the purchase at 63 dollars would be in a loss position.

The decision to buy, sell or hold depends on the individual investor's situation. Many active investors would take the loss at the 10 to 15 percent level and move on to other opportunities. Serious consideration should be given to the strategy best suited to risk tolerance and previously established investment strategies.

Losing stocks demand a careful strategy. Whether the strategy is to sell the stock and buy another, or build up an investment position in the losing stock, the investor should always act quickly. If the stock is completely researched and planned ahead of time, it will be easier to put the preplanned strategy to work.

Chapter 4

It Is Better to Average Up Than to Average Down

Price averaging can be a prudent strategy with the right stock and situation. There are two ways to lower the average cost basis of the investment. One is averaging up as was discussed earlier and the other is averaging down (buying more of the same stock at lower prices). If an investor is caught by a sudden decline in stock price, it might be worthwhile to hold on to the original investment, let the price drop until it bottoms out and then begin a program of buying in at various price levels as the stock moves up.

Averaging down, though frequently suggested, is often not the best course of action. It can work in certain specific situations, but it won't fit well into most investment plans. It is an ultra-aggressive strategy, which some would describe as "throwing good money after bad." Although the strategy is sometimes effective with drops in lower priced stocks (such as 15 dollar a share and less), there is no way to know how low the price will drop or when it will recover.

Implementation of an averaging down strategy can also be difficult. Few investors would have the discipline to buy more stock at regular intervals as the price is declining. The strategy might be easy to follow once or twice, but can become more and more difficult as the stock continues to drop in price.

A strategy that can lower the average price of a stock, with less risk than averaging down, can be accomplished by averaging up. Earlier a method of averaging up was explained as a strategy to enhance the profits on an advancing stock. This second method of averaging up relates to a stock that is currently in a losing position.

Averaging up can be more emotionally difficult than buying a winner, but it can also be effective by increasing profits. It is an aggressive strategy, not without risk, although it is possible to place some limitations on that risk.

When the stock an investor is holding suddenly takes a turn for the worse and the price declines significantly due to a bad market or bad news, the investor could decide to hold and see how low the price is able to drop. Eventually the stock will reach a support level and buyers will stop the fall. If the investor believes the stock holds value, in spite of the selling which has occurred, it can be an ideal time to begin averaging up.

Take a look at the Dayton Hudson stock. If an investor had purchased 100 shares at 63 dollars per share in October of 1987, things could have been difficult. As the bottom dropped out of the market and Dayton Hudson also plunged in price, the investor decided that the company was still sound and would be likely to recover. Also, the investor had the assets to begin a strategy of averaging up once the price became stable.

The investor believed that the stock would move a few points up as new buyers were attracted, so decided to make use of "buy stop" orders (an order placed above the current price that becomes a market order as the stock trades at or through the stop price). In this way the investor is only buying more stock if the price is rising. If the price falls back, the buy stop orders are not filled, but the position is held.

Will Rogers had a stock like this in mind when he said, ". . . only buy the stock which goes up. If it don't go up, don't buy it."

The belief is that the stock will recover, the strategy of only buying if the stock rises and the action of placing the buy stop orders are in line with each other.

Original Purchase 100 Shares At $63.00 = $6,300.00

	Buy Stop	Quantity New/Total	Fill Price	Average Price	Total Invested
1.	$25.00	100/200	$25.25	$44.125	$ 8,825
2.	$30.00	100/300	$30.00	$39.41	$11,825
3.	$35.00	100/400	$35.00	$38.31	$15,325
4.	$40.00	100/500	$40.75	$38.80	$19,400
5.	$45.00	100/600	$45.00	$39.83	$23,900

(Notice the average price drops in transactions 1, 2, and 3. It then begins to rise, but is still significantly below the current market price.)

The high price for 1988 was 45.5. If the investor sold the 600 shares at 45 dollars a share, there would be a profit of more than 3,000 dollars. If the investor waited until the summer of 1989 and sold at 60 dollars a share (still 3 dollars *under* the original purchase price) the investor would show a profit of 12,102 dollars. On an initial investment of 23,900 dollars that is a return of more than 50 percent, which is a reasonable return on an investment in any portfolio.

Average Cost Per Share =	$39.83
Sell Price =	60.00
Profits Per Share =	20.17

$$\frac{\text{Profit Per Share } \$20.17}{\text{Average Cost Per } \$39.83} = 50.64\% \text{ Total Gain}$$

Averaging up has the advantage, for the investor, of making moves only on the price recovery of the stock. It is more comfortable for investors to add funds to a stock that is rising in price rather than buying a stock declining in price.

Buy stop orders should be fully understood before making the move and the protection of limits should be seriously considered. However, the strategy makes sound investment

sense and the investor is more likely to stay with the implementation.

Notice the results would have yielded even greater profits
if the purchase of 400 shares had been implemented all at
once, at the low price. This is a valid point. It would also
have been a strategy with higher risk, the stock might not
have recovered. Even though this would appear to have been
an excellent strategy, no investor is able to see into the future.
If earnings had tumbled after the price drop, recovery could
have taken several years.

Although buying stock is gambling on future results, it is
prudent and sensible to set a strategy that limits risk whenever
possible. By averaging up with a strategy using buy stops and
limits, the investor has some control of the risk. In this way
the investor is acting on observable recovery.

Chapter 5

Good Companies Buy Their Own Stock

"XYZ Company has announced a purchase of two million shares of their own stock. The stock must be a good buy if the company itself is willing to buy the stock!"

This is a common belief. It is sometimes a selling point used by stockbrokers. The stockbroker tells a client, that investor tells a friend and so on. Many of these and other investors rush out to purchase more of the stock, causing the price to rise significantly during the next few days.

Actually, the company stock purchase announcement can be a bit of a "mixed bag," with some good news and other not necessarily good news. This timing of the stock repurchase might be set to soften the blow of other, negative information being released. The "good news . . . bad news" technique is often used, even by some of the largest corporations, to give a positive boost to the price of the stock. The strategy can be effective enough to cause the stock price to rise significantly even though the bad news is serious.

At times, the stock buy back is only an announcement with no stock purchase ever taking place. There might have originally been a stock purchase intended but financing ran into difficulties and the money just isn't available. Companies are occasionally accused of trumpeting a stock buy back for the purpose of supporting or accelerating the price of the stock. While this is possible in some situations, the large majority of stock buy back activities are sincere.

There can be many reasons for a company to buy their own stock. Stock purchases by companies are generally looked on as a positive sign if a company has purchased the stock on a regular basis or if a substantial buy back of shares is announced, such as 5 percent, 10 percent or more. This is particularly true with the small to medium size company.

William J. O'Neil describes the positive effects this way:

"This reduces the number of shares of common stock in the capital structure and implies the corporation expects improved   sales and earnings in the future...total company earnings will, as a result, usually be divided among a smaller number of shares, which will automatically increase the earnings per share."[1]

Toward the end of April, 1989, Union Pacific announced a major restructuring which included a plan to buy back as much as 13 percent of its outstanding common stock. The stock, which had been languishing, immediately responded and soared $5.25 to a level of $71.375 per share. The stock gained new strength and kept on moving upward with the stock market.

Buying back 13 percent of Union Pacific stock certainly was a positive move for the price of the stock. Other positive restructuring moves were also announced. They were a combination of divestiture and acquisition moves which had the intent of making the company more profitable for the long term. If the restructuring continues and earnings keep increasing, the price of the stock will likely react accordingly in an upward direction.

There are several reasons for a company to buy back its own stock. Some are positive from the investors viewpoint, others are not.

---

1   *How to Make Money in Stocks*, by William J. O'Neil, published by McGraw-Hill, 1988, p. 31.

Price Movement Chart: Union Pacific

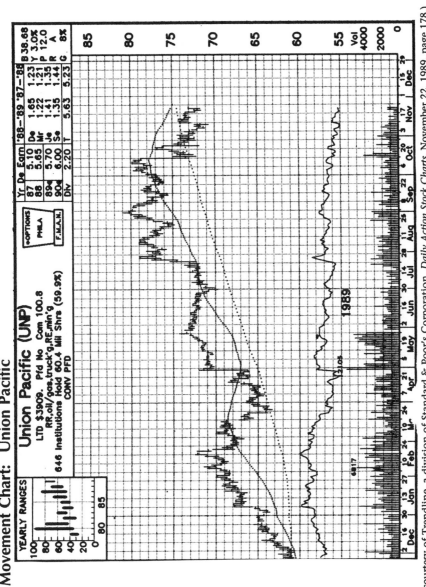

(Chart courtesy of Trendline, a division of Standard & Poor's Corporation. *Daily Action Stock Charts*, November 22, 1989, page 178.)

The stock is undervalued at the current price: Undervalued simply means the company has greater inherent value than is reflected in the current market price. This "undervalued" statement might be part of the announcement concerning the buy back. It could actually be the reason behind the action. If so, it is a very positive sign for the future of the stock. However, it is important to remember that the company, which is buying its own stock, can usually afford to hold that stock for a longer period of time than the investor is willing to wait for a profit.

The company might need stock for employee purchase plans: This is certainly not a negative reason for the buy back, but it isn't necessarily a positive reason either. Companies need a certain amount of stock for their employee purchase plans (pension or non-pension). The employee is usually allowed to buy the stock at a predetermined amount below current market price. The timing is likely based on the companies' need for stock rather than the current market price of the stock. This is a rather neutral reason for the company to buy it's own stock.

The company could be accumulating stock in order to leverage a buy out and go private: The accumulation would tend to nudge the price upward at a fairly regular pace. This announcement would not likely be made until the company had purchased a significant quantity of its own stock. This would tend to be a positive for the stockholder, for the short-term gain.

The company could be building a defense against a takeover. This could lead to a nasty takeover battle. The company could win but end up with significant debt. Takeover battles can end up in a "greenmail" situation, where the company is forced to borrow money to buy back stock from an unfriendly suitor.

Unocal (formerly Union Oil Company) had this experience in the mid 1980s. The company had to take on extensive debt to ward off an acquisition. The price suffered by going from a high of 53 in 1985 to a low of 15.6 in 1986. It took until 1989 to climb up near the former highs.

The announcement of a stock buy back can have many implications. In most cases this is a positive move for the company and the stockholders, mainly due to the improvement in earnings per share since there will be fewer shares outstanding. A stock will often rise after such an announcement, but it can certainly begin to fall in a short time if negative news emerges or the earnings begin to weaken.

In an upward moving stock market a stock buy back can be a buying signal, even if the investor is too late for the initial price increase. There is a strong motivation for the stock to rise even higher. This can also be a reason to increase the size of the position in a stock the individual investor already owns. It can be an ideal time to buy more shares. Also, the event can be a valid reason for raising a sell price objective to a higher price, because the buy back instantly raises the per share earnings.

Although a stock repurchase announcement can be positive news in any stock market, rising or falling, some analysis of the reasons behind the action can determine the validity of the buy back and its potential effect on the price of the stock.

The investor should follow up to see if the stock is actually repurchased as per the announcement. One can watch the newspapers for the announcement or call the company (investor relations) and ask when the buy back will occur.

If the actual repurchase is only partially accomplished or totally non-existent, the investor would do well to reconsider the position. If an investor is considering an original stock purchase, based on a stock buy back situation, it could be good to see what kind of a move the stock has already made.

Chapter 6

Watch Out for Block Trades

Block trading of 5,000, 10,000 or 20,000 shares or more will appear, in the statistics for individual stocks, during the trading day. Mutual Funds, Insurance Companies, Pension Funds or other institutional investors are changing their investment positions.

The question arises, are they buying or selling these large blocks of stock? Although there might be some situations where the blocks are buys, such as buyout scenarios or other possible "arbitrage plays," block trades tend to be the selling of stock.

The stock has been accumulated in smaller segments. In fact the stock might have been accumulated through a buying program of "averaging up." When the sell occurs the institutional investor does not want to take the time to unload the stock in small segments, as this could drive the price lower, so it is sold as a block trade of 10,000 or more shares.

William J. O'Neil, of *Investor's Daily* newspaper has this to say about block trades:

> In today's institutionally dominated markets, large numbers of big blocks of stock trade every day. Many of these blocks of 10,000 to 500,000 shares or more are crossed by block houses (institutional brokerage firms specializing in large transactions).

Sometimes they represent both sides of the order, acting as broker for both the buyer and seller. In certain of these cases it may be of value to know if a stock exchange specialist has taken any stock in position on the block trade.

Block houses positioning (buying for their own trading account) a block that trades on a big down tick from the prior trade will try to dispose of their stock as soon as possible over the next few trading days. Block trades unchanged or only 1/8 of a point above or below the prior trade are confusing and misleading to the public and are sucker bait for the uninitiated. Arbitrage and deliberate painting of the tape by crossing blocks that are being sold on 1/8 of a point up ticks complicate the analysis of large transactions.[1]

Studying block trades can be a way to observe the institutional interest in a stock. If a significant number of block trades are occurring on down ticks, the institutions could be pulling their assets out and the stock could decline in price. On the other hand, if block trades are occurring on up ticks, the stock might be becoming a target. Information on block trades is listed in the daily financial news.

Block trading is probably best observed as one more indicator of a possible change in the market or individual stocks. It, most definitely, signifies an increase of activity and interest, although it is sometimes difficult to read as positive or negative.

---

1   *How to Make Money in Stocks*, by William J. O'Neil, published by McGraw-Hill Book Company, 1988, p. 199, 200.

Chapter 7

Look for Insider's Trading

Insiders of a corporation are the decision makers and the strategy formulators. They are the directors, the officers and the high level "line" personnel. If anyone knows what is going on in a particular company, it is the managers who are directly involved in the decision-making process.

Although there are usually restrictions in their trading of the company stock, the insiders are allowed to do some buying and selling of that stock. Some of the financial news media (such as *The Wall Street Journal*, or *Investor's Daily*) as well as various newsletters publish figures of "insider" buys and sells.[1] This information is often as much as a week or a month or more old, but can give some insight as to executive accumulation of a particular stock. The most complete source of insider's trading is put out by the Securities and Exchange Commission.[2]

---

1   *The Insider Transactions Report*, published by Mark Les, P. O. Box 1145, Costa Mesa, CA 92628. Phone (800) 333-2019.

2   Called the *Official Summary of Securities Transactions and Holdings* and is put out monthly. However, it is not the most timely information as it appears three to four months after the transactions. More timely information can be obtained from *Insider's Chronicle,* published by Transamerica Media Corp., and *Vickers Weekly Insider Report,* published by Vickers Stock Research Corp.

Investors with a personal computer can subscribe to services which will actually monitor insider trading activities with complete details. These on-line services can be part of a package deal, combined with other services, or can be an independent program. As personal computer trading is becoming popular more brokerage firms are offering programs which include detailed information on insider transactions. If one has access to a personal computer, with modem, this information is easily accessible.[3]

Insider's trading is quite different from "insider trading." Insider's trading is the activity of corporate officers and other executives who buy and sell stock in the companies that employ them. On the other hand, "insider trading" is the buying and selling of securities based on information that has not yet been released to the general public. The important difference is that insider's trading is legal and trading on inside information is illegal.

This is as true for company insiders as it is for anyone who buys and sells stock. As has been observed in the past few years illegal insider trading can and does occur. The Securities Exchange Commission has been more diligent in curtailing the occurrence of these illegal activities, although it is a difficult activity to control.

At times insider's trading shows nothing of significance. In the summer of 1989 two important corporate takeovers appeared with NWA Corp. and UAL Corporation. NWA Corp. showed no significant insider buys or sells and UAL Corp. showed a total of three insider buys and one insider sell.

The months involved were October, November, December of 1988 and the sell in January of 1989. The buys were significant as they reflected the price strength which had been increasing for the entire year of 1988. The bidding action for UAL Corp. didn't really get rolling until August of 1989, therefore the buys were a positive indicator for the earnings

---

3   Vickers On-Line, 226 New York Avenue, Huntington, NY 11743 (516) 423-7710.

and future of UAL Corp., rather than an indication of an approaching suitor. One sell does not appear to be meaningful.

In these cases the records of insider transactions were of little significance. This is partly due to the fact that even the corporate executives do not often see a buy out approaching. NWA Corp. had recently completed an extensive study which indicated that a takeover was unlikely due to the potential difficulties with the various unions involved. This illustrates what a waste of time such studies can be. In fact it makes one wonder if the "take over study" was a sort of flag waving which was actually trying to attract the attentions of an acceptable suitor.

When an investor is building and managing a stock portfolio, two situations can arise in which the trades of insiders can be significant.

A Rise in Insider Buys: This phenomenon should be noted when selecting a stock. A sudden flurry of insider buys can be a positive statement of the earnings and growth potential of the company.

Media Attention: If the insider's trading has been significant enough to be discussed in one of the financial news media, it calls additional attention to the activity. This only occurs if a fairly large amount of activity has been noticed.

Obviously an investor can also follow insider's trading as an investment strategy by itself. This strategy should be researched ahead of time in order to develop some understanding of the effects of insider's trading on the prices of different stocks.

Insider Sells vs. Insider Purchases

Insider sells are often not particularly meaningful as an activity indicator. Insider sells are often activities which raise cash to purchase items other than stock. A new car, boat or a down payment on a new lake cabin are often the motivating influences on insider sales of stock.

An exception to the concept of insider selling being insignificant is when there is an extraordinary amount of selling activity. Again, if there is enough insider selling to cause a news item the stock will likely react with volatility.

On September 6, 1989, *The Wall Street Journal* published an article regarding heavy insider selling in the stock of Liz Claiborne. The article reported that five insiders, including the chairman and president had been selling significant blocks of stock since May of 1989. The stock which had closed at 27 dollars a share on Tuesday was significantly effected by the news, closing at a price of 25 7/8 -1 1/8 on Wednesday. By Thursday, September 14, the stock was trading at 24 1/4.

Even though various market analysts were stating the financial condition of Liz Claiborne was a positive buying opportunity, sellers reacted to the news. This was a situation which could go either way. If the analysts were correct, Liz Claiborne could become a screaming buy. If the inside sellers were correct, the stock was a definite sell.

In most cases the selling by insiders is not this significant. Even in the Liz Claiborne situation, one of the insiders indicated that the sell was determined by the expiration of the holding period required from purchasing the stock through company options. The proceeds were to primarily be used to pay for the original option exercise.

Six months later, Liz Claiborne was trading at 26 dollars a share. Not much price appreciation nor depreciation. Investors were possibly still wondering what to do with the stock.

Purchases by insiders are another matter. Open market purchases (stocks not purchased through the company) are more significant than company sponsored stock option purchases. When the insider is buying stock on the open market it is without the favorable price incentives of the stock option plan. This suggests a strong positive belief in the immediate future of the company's profits.

Insider purchases are relatively common. In fact there appear to be scattered insider purchases occurring much of the

time, therefore it can be advantageous for the investor to pa-
tiently assess the situation over a period of weeks and months.
In the words of Aaron B. Feigen, CFA, President of The Insider Reports Fund: "Repeated behavior stretched over a long
period of time is usually more important than concentrated
trading during a short time span." [4]

The analysis should involve looking for patterns or trends
developing, rather than jumping to conclusions with isolated
insider transactions.

At times the amount of shares being purchased, as well
as the number of insiders doing the purchasing, will dramatically increase. This can be significant and worth further inves-
tigation. The stock price will generally react swiftly (upward)
and be difficult to take advantage of if the investor wishes to
be a buyer. Many investors are not put off by the sudden
price increase as these insider transactions are often indicative
of positive longer term trends as well. Therefore, the investor
can take advantage of the situation as a long-term trader of
stock.

Some guidelines in the assessment of insider trades can
be helpful. D. Robert Coulson in his book *The Intelligent
Investor's Guide to Profiting from Stock Market Inefficiencies*
suggests a set of guidelines which can be helpful.

Since approximately 200-300 insider transactions are reported weekly by these services, a method of selecting from
among the many stocks involved in insider's trading is needed.
The following are some guidelines that you may use in selecting inside-traded stocks for purchase:

- Purchases by only chief executive officers, chairmen
  of boards of directors or directors should be considered (Officer-directors are usually not tabulated as
  such in the newsletters.)

---

4   *Investing With the Insiders Legally,* published by Simon & Schuster,
     Inc., 1988, page 109.

- Stocks that have experienced recent insider selling should not be selected.
- Stocks that have been purchased by more than one preferred insider (CEO or DIR) should be preferred.
- Count as purchases only those that are open-market purchases.
- Token purchases (less than about 5–10 percent of holdings) should be ignored.
- All else equal, choose stocks having the most recent transactions dates.[5]

Insider buying is considered a positive signal by many stock traders. The purchases might be caused by several factors:

- A general increase in business which might not yet be reflected in an earnings report.
- A change in company policy.
- The emergence from a difficult situation which could have a positive impact on future earnings.
- A price level in the stock which appears to be under-valued. (Some insiders know the value of the company's stock and know it well.)
- The presence of positive rumors. (As takeover rumors begin to run through a company grapevine, many believe that it is only a matter of time until a takeover actually does occur.)

Many insider purchases are small and insignificant. It can be difficult to tell if the purchases are significant. Again, Dr.

---

5   *The Intelligent Investor's Guide to Profiting from Stock Market Inefficiencies*, by D. Robert Coulson, Ph.D. Published by Probus Publishing Co. 1987, p. 109, 110.

Coulson has a suggested guideline. "Another guideline that is often suggested for selecting insider stocks is the 'minimum purchase' guideline. I recommend that you consider only trades of $20,000 or more as meaningful insider trades."[6]

There are a couple of important insider selling situations which should raise a feeling of caution. Situations which include directors who are consistently selling stock and smaller companies announcing an important principal has recently left and gone elsewhere.

If more than one or two directors are selling consistently, they might be leaving. This could have an impact on the operations of the company. Even if the change will be a better situation for the company, the stock could experience significant selling.

If the company is rather small in size (for example 200 million or less in annual sales) and a President or important Vice President leaves with a significantly large volume of stock (250 thousand or 500 thousand shares), a problem can develop with the price of the stock. When this person begins to sell that stock the price can be driven down to a significantly lower level. These situations can force any institutions currently holding the stock to also sell. When the institutions leave, the price recovery can be slow and difficult.

For example, in 1986 a small (less than five million shares) company known as Grist Mill encountered a similar occurrence. Grist Mill was at the time manufacturing granola bars and fruit snacks. They had some weakness in earnings, but were realigning their efforts to correct the situation.

The announcement came that a principal employee of the company left, still owning reportedly 250,000 shares of common stock. This was stock which was not restricted in any way. It could be sold all at once or in small quantities. The stock began selling in blocks of 10,000 shares and the price of the stock started to drop. Institutions became nervous and

---

6   Ibid.

began unloading their positions. The stock continued to drop in price.

Grist Mill, in 1986, had a high price of 13 1/2 dollars a share and a low of 1/2. That was significant price damage. The price recovery was slow, but definite. Things were a bit better in 1987 with a high of 4 3/8 and a low of 1 7/8. 1988 saw the stock recover to 10 5/8.

The company was beginning to look good again and became a viable trading stock. The point is a lot of potential profit was lost by those buyers at 13 1/2. Granted they would be in good shape by hanging on to the stock, but they would have to wait nearly three years. The institutional investors gradually came back to the stock as buyers and in 1989 Grist Mill was trading at more than 15 dollars a share. The stock had recovered.

Obviously it could have been a good buy at less than a dollar a share, but the problem is companies rarely recover from such battered price levels. This is important because it is often the smaller companies which show greater returns following insider purchases. Therefore, they can become an excellent target for the more speculative stock trader.

Analyzing insiders trades can be profitable information in some cases. Buys by insiders are usually more meaningful than sells, however some large sells or multiple sells can serve as a warning signal to the investor.

Chapter 8

Buy Low—Sell High

Charles Dow, one of the founding fathers of Dow Jones & Company and first editor of *The Wall Street Journal,* might have put it this way:

Buy a stock which has value in earnings and value in the dividend paid out. As this stock rises in price and the value of earnings and dividends declines, sell the stock.

Although the methods of evaluating stock "of value" have changed, the basic idea is still sound. The anticipation of value and value increase are what makes a stock rise in price. The value is not in the price alone, but rather in the factors that make the stock an attractive purchase. A primary factor of value in today's market is earnings, earnings past and future, due to the tendency of stocks to trade on the anticipation of earnings increases.

This idea is as old as trading ownership of properties. It is the basis of all business. Buy a property at one price and sell it at a higher price. The money between the difference of the buy and sell transaction is called profit. This is the reason for buying and selling stock. To make a profit.

There is a phenomena in the stock market which appears to be just the opposite. Many individual investors make the mistake of buying stock when it is high priced and rising, then sell the stock as the price drops. Their actions suggest they believe that value is found in the price alone. Although they aren't right all the time, professional stock traders tend to trade the sequence more correctly by buying the stock when it is lower in price (but higher in value) and selling for profit as the price rises.

Although this idea appears simple, in the real world of trading stocks it can be difficult to determine when a stock is either "low" or "high." When the emotions of hope, greed and fear become involved, this simple concept becomes complicated and confused. It becomes difficult to not be lured into buying a fast rising stock in hopes that the price will continue to rise. On the other hand it is difficult, emotionally, to want to hold on to a stock that is continuing downward in price.

Take a look at the twelve month chart for American Stores (ASC). It can be easy to say buy at 54 dollars and sell at 71, but when the stock was at 54 it could have gone to 50 or lower.

As far as selling at 71 is concerned, it is obvious that the buyers were looking for greater earnings which failed to occur. In fact a look at the earnings makes one wonder why this stock even rallied to above 70 dollars a share.

Twelve-month earnings of 2.30 dollars a share versus 3.77 dollars a share the previous year are difficult to get excited about. This stock has become a "turnaround" situation and has not yet made that all-important turn. Even the five-year rate in earnings of -14 percent say that the corner might be a long ways away. When this stock builds some stability in the earnings trend buyers will likely return.

Look at a price movement chart for Maytag Corporation.

The peaks and valleys are easily observed. Any investor would like to have bought Maytag stock in the early part of January 1989, and sold the stock in the last week of August. Anyone who could have pulled off that short-term strategy would have an enviable profit in the stock. This is a stock which was showing some weakness in earnings for the first two quarters of the year (March, 35 cents vs. 43 cents and June, 27 cents vs. 47 cents).

In those days of late August, early September, Maytag Corp. was trading at a P/E ratio (price to earnings) of 17.7. It is difficult to know if this is high or low, without looking at some history.

Price Movement Chart: Maytag Corporation

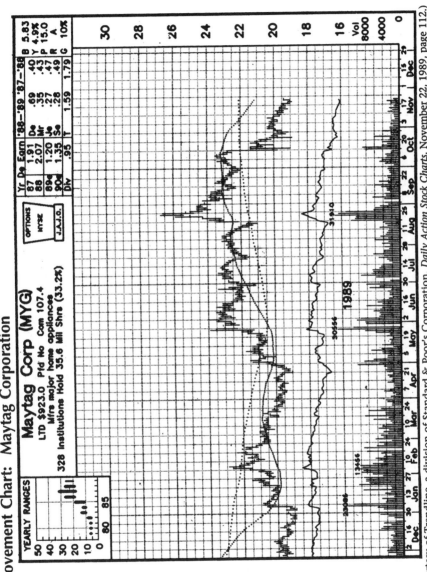

(Chart courtesy of Trendline, a division of Standard & Poor's Corporation. *Daily Action Stock Charts*, November 22, 1989, page 112.)

Price Movement Chart: American Stores

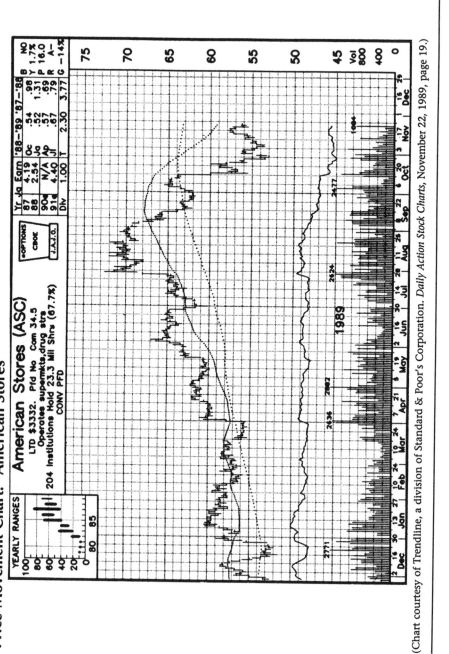

(Chart courtesy of Trendline, a division of Standard & Poor's Corporation. *Daily Action Stock Charts*, November 22, 1989, page 19.)

From time to time there are various debates heard on the value of the P/E ratios. Peter Lynch, former portfolio manager of Fidelity's Magellan Fund has this to say of the ratio of discussion: "Before you buy a stock, you might want to track its P/E ratio back through several years to get a sense of normal levels."

The price/earnings ratio of Maytag was about 12 at the time of the price movement chart. Earlier it had been above 17. If we take a look at the P/E ratio history for Maytag Corporation it looks like this:

Year	P/E Ratio
1989	15.0
1988	13.0
1987	13.5
1986	14.7
1985	10.4
1984	9.4
1983	11.1
1982	11.0
1981	10.1
1980	9.5

Considering the weakness in earnings in the early part of 1989, and the historically high price/earnings ratio in September, it is not too surprising to see the price of the stock go to lower levels. Many investors considered it overpriced and sold their positions. It appears to be the change from historic levels rather than the P/E ratio itself that has greatest significance in the movement of a stock's price.

If the price drops low enough and the earnings remain constant or increase, Maytag Corp. could be considered an "undervalued" stock. This is when buyers generally return and push the stock price higher.

Price Movement Chart: Nike

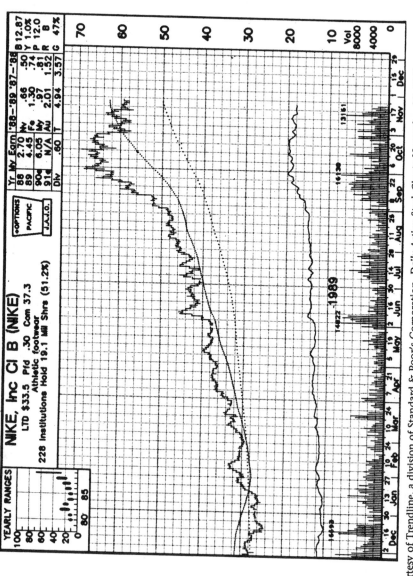

(Chart courtesy of Trendline, a division of Standard & Poor's Corporation. *Daily Action Stock Charts*, November 22, 1989, page 127.)

Nike is an example of a stock which was slow to rally on good news in February. An increase in earnings from 74 cents a share to 1.30 is significant. It represents a 75 percent increase in earnings. The stock showed a modest increase from the 28 dollar range to the 32 dollar range, a 14 percent increase in price. Many were tempted to sell and take profits. The stock drifted lower, toward 30 dollars a share. That was when the momentum began, carrying the stock to nearly 70 dollars a share. A 250 percent increase! Should the investor sell? Maybe not.

The given year growth shows a 47 percent five-year earnings growth rate, the stock has shown a twelve-month earnings growth rate of nearly 40 percent. This could become even greater.

This could be the time to place the stop loss order. If the stock drops due to profit taking and the sell stop order is activated and the stock sold, the investor might want to buy the same stock again. This is assuming a stability of growth in earnings.

One of the important keys to trading stock is to be aware of its current value in relation to earnings. This relationship is often the cause of price movement. Stock will often rise in anticipation of an increase in value and fall on the reality, when the expectations have changed.

The maxim of "buy low, sell high" is a generality which conveys the basic principle of taking profits, but provides no strategy for dealing with growth in the price of a stock. Perhaps the maxim would be more helpful if it said:

- Buy Low in Relation to Earnings (low price, high earnings).
- Protect Significant Profits.
- Sell When Change Occurs and Earnings Become Weak in Relation to the Price (high price, low earnings).

When should profits be taken?

As long as the price is continuing to grow and has a fundamental (earnings and price growth related) reason to keep growing, a sell price objective should be raised. A sell of Nike at 68 dollars a share could be making a big mistake. An investor who is "stopped out" of Nike at 60 dollars a share on a profit-taking correction has a great profit to reinvest—in Nike (on another profit-taking correction) or in some other great stock.

A little research is in order, when being tempted to sell and take profits, a study of earnings growth and historic P/E ratios can provide a different strategy. When the investor looks at current value, the time might be right to actually buy more of the same stock and increase the position.

Determining what "low" and "high" actually mean, by the analysis of the earnings and earnings growth, price patterns and price/earnings ratio history can help the individual investor determine the timing for buying and selling stocks. The research can provide a good picture of the current value of the stock and provide the investor with buy and sell target prices. This is a more realistic approach than basing decisions on the amount of profit the investor wishes to earn.[1]

---

1   *One Up on Wall Street* by Peter Lynch. Published by Simon and Schuster, 1989, page 165.

Chapter 9

Buy High—Sell Higher

Many individuals attempt to "buy high and sell higher" when buying a stock that is running up in price. It is a strategy also used by professional traders. However, professional traders are the experts, their career depends on making good judgments most of the time.

Professional stock traders have certain advantages over individual investors. Not only do they have access to the best news and research available, they have the dollar resources to make large trades, with very low commission rates, for modest gains. Institutional traders can trade a stock for a quarter or even an eighth. The individual investor usually needs more of a gain to cover the cost of commission and make a reasonable profit.

The biggest disadvantage to professional stock traders is the absolute necessity of trading. They usually can't sell all of their stock and put the money in a bank or money market fund. They have to keep trading stocks. This can be an advantage to the individual investor. All that is necessary is to figure out where the professional is likely to go with the next investment. Granted, the large trader can develop a significant cash position in a weak market, but the astute individual can either sell and get out early or hold on to the stock and ride out the storm.

A strong market decline creates lower prices and large cash positions, the earnings of the stocks can remain unchanged (this means their value has increased as the prices dropped). The bargains can only be resisted for a limited time. The climb back to former levels might take a few months or longer, but the recovery will come in time.

The individual investor should endeavor to seek out the kinds of stocks which either are in play by the institutions or will likely come into play. These are usually the stocks that have a strong price and earnings performance record and are in an industry with identified growth potential. A company that makes flying broomsticks might have a lot of potential, but it is difficult to imagine, qualify and quantify market demand for the product.

Conversely, consider a company like Medtronic, which has been a leader in the medical device industry for many years. The company virtually created the heart pacemaker industry. As an industry leader, the company has done well in the past few years. As earnings have done well, increasing the value of the stock, the price has adjusted in an upward direction.

Take a look at the price movement for Medtronic stock. A glance at the twelve month S&P chart shows that Medtronic, Inc. is on a bit of a plateau, similar to a plateau that existed back in June of 1989. The move up from June was strong. The stock moved from the 48 to 49 dollar per share range up to the low sixties (prices adjusted for 2 for 1 split). This was a 20 percent price increase in just over two months. If an investor became interested in the stock during the last two weeks of August, how would it be possible to "buy low"?

If the investor decided to wait for a sign of price weakness, it would eventually arrive in mid-September, but it is likely that 10 percent or more of the rapid growth would have been missed. The advantage to buying as the stock was moving was greater profits resulting from the probable anticipation of earnings growth and a positive 2 for 1 stock split. An advantage in waiting until the end of September was current information; i.e., September chart and earnings information.

Price Movement Chart: Medtronic, Inc.

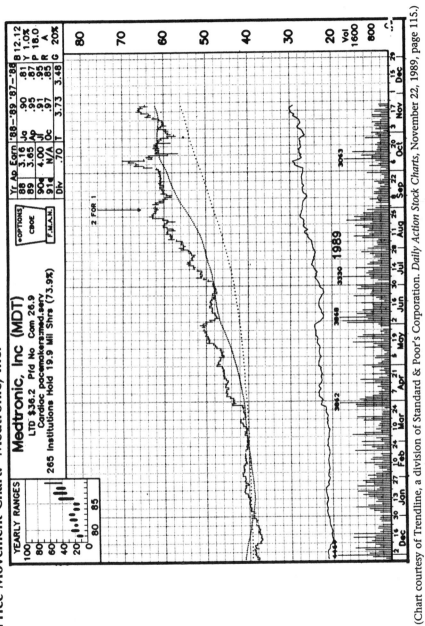

(Chart courtesy of Trendline, a division of Standard & Poor's Corporation. *Daily Action Stock Charts*, November 22, 1989, page 115.)

The strategy of buy high/sell higher can be enhanced by anticipated increases in earnings or corporate takeover situations. The anticipation of earnings growth will create higher P/E ratios—high in relation to historic levels, other companies in the same industry and the market as a whole (such as the average P/E ratio of the S&P 500 or the Dow Industrials). Stocks with higher P/E ratios will generally become volatile in price swings as the earnings growth anticipation is either being fulfilled or turning to disappointment.

Corporate takeover situations are a different situation. Many professional arbitragers go on search missions in which they look specifically for companies likely to be bought out by some other company. In the late 1980s there have been several large LBO (Leveraged Buy Out) situations. The LBO can become a classic Buy High/Sell Higher situation. In 1988 and 1989 it seemed as though money-heavy corporations would rather invest in the market by purchasing an entire company than by investing in the stock of several different companies. To those who could afford it, this strategy proposed the existence of more profit and less risk in buying an entire company rather than investing in the stock market.

Although there can be considerable risk involved, nearly every buy-out situation is accompanied by a drop in stock price relatively soon after the announcement. The profit takers, whether nervous nellies or prudent investors will take the profit that presents itself and sell the stock. Many will not wait for the final deal to be consummated.

Two important takeover situations in the summer of 1989 were NWA (Northwest Airlines) Corporation and UAL (United Airlines) Corporation. The interesting battle was the bidding war that evolved over NWA, because it appeared to create another situation with UAL. The investment group, led by Al Checchi, won the battle over the first announced bidder, Marvin Davis. This obviously left Mr. Davis with a "War Chest" of capital with which to invest. Logic dictated that Davis would invest in an airline, since he had become well acquainted with this type of investment in the preceding months.

Such decisions are not made lightly. They involve the necessary analysis and decision making which are an essential portion of the investment. One might even conclude that Mr. Davis's team had a secondary target from the beginning. That target became UAL after the NWA deal went to someone else. It is also possible that the UAL deal was actually the primary target, with the first acquisition (on NWA) being a ruse to lure a competitive bidder.

Several bidders appeared on the scene, including one of the employee unions, all stating an intention to buy out UAL Corp. The price continued to soar and hardly anyone noticed the original bidder quietly slip into the background.

Look at the three distinct "corrections" that took place in July and August. They don't appear to be severe when taken in context with the full picture, but when they occurred they became tempting sell signals to many nervous investors. Any stop loss orders placed in this area became fair game for the speculators. Large investors know that sell stop orders will be placed about 10 percent lower than the current price. At times, these investors will institute sell programs to force the stock's price down. As the price drops it begins to activate the sell stop orders and the stock price will often free fall a few more dollars. When the stock has fallen to a support level (a price that brings buyers of the stock) these same investors will then begin to rebuy the stock, at bargain prices.

It should be mentioned that the UAL acquisition was not a done deal at the end of September; in fact it was still up in the air (so to speak) into 1990. The price, which was pushing 300 dollars a share during the heat of the action, eventually dropped by half that amount. During the first part of May 1990, the price of UAL stock was 153 dollars a share—an unpleasant development for the many investors who were still holding on to the stock they purchased at 200 to 300 dollars per share.

Price Movement Chart: UAL Corporation

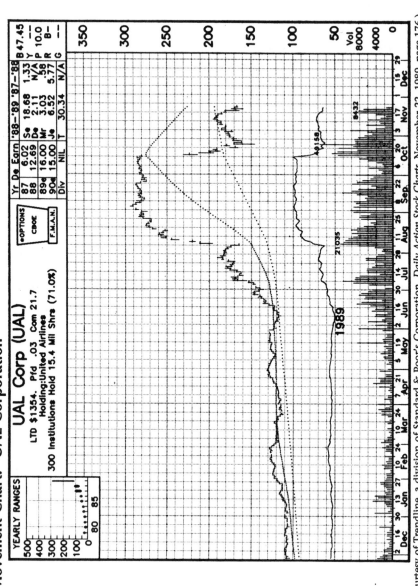

(Chart courtesy of Trendline, a division of Standard & Poor's Corporation. *Daily Action Stock Charts*, November 22, 1989, page 176.)

This type of situation can be frustrating to the investor. For a number of reasons, not all takeover situations materialize:

- the bidders could back out at the last moment,
- the current corporate management might arrive at a successful anti-takeover strategy,
- financing can become difficult or impossible,
- unions might bring a halt to the proceedings, or
- something unforeseen can occur to stop the takeover.

Any halt or hesitation of the proceedings can easily result in a loss for the investor who is late on the scene.

Buying high and selling higher can be a viable way to make money in the stock market, but it is not without risk. The strategy is one which usually calls for the intention of a long-term hold. Many investors attempt to buy high and sell higher on a short-term basis, only to be whipsawed by a volatile situation in the market or with the individual stock. They often buy the stock after a strong price advance and then turn around and sell it as the price drops to former levels. What these investors do not realize is that a stock is not necessarily a loser just because the price is dropping to a former trading range.

Corporate takeovers that fail to materialize are a bit of a different story. If the buy out does not occur, the stock will generally fall back to previous levels and below. If an investor has bought the stock near the top of the price advance, it will probably work out best to sell, take the loss and be done with it before it gets any worse.

Stocks caught up in the acquisition frenzy are frequently whipped back and forth by arbs (those trading for arbitrage), corporate raiders or newly formed buying groups. Their intent is simple, make money on the price fluctuations. This means they are literally taking money away from someone else. The stocks caught in this game of buying and selling are in for a bumpy ride as far as price is concerned. The actual earnings become rather meaningless and it is the play in the stock which is exciting. This is generally not a favorable investment climate for the inexperienced investor. The prices can move from outrageously high to absurdly low in a short period of time.

Sometimes the play is carried on with a relatively low-priced stock. An arbitrage player can make a profit on a quarter or an eighth of a dollar. If a stock is gyrating between 2 1/2 to 3 dollars a share it can become the target of the players. The individuals in such cases are often the losers.

Chapter 10

Buy On the Rumor— Sell On the News

An old saw that usually accompanies the buy high/sell higher strategy is to ". . . buy on the rumor, sell on the news." This can be an effective strategy in many ways, but the investor must be willing to accept certain conditions. For instance, the rumor might have been fabricated with the intent of pushing the stock price up.

Financial consultants, whether they are advisors or stock-brokers, tend to discourage those who would buy any stock based on rumor alone. In the past couple of years there have been many false rumors regarding corporate takeover situations. The stocks quickly retreated to former levels. In most cases it is best to leave the rumor alone.

There are many instances in which "selling on the news" would have been premature: a couple of years ago Firestone had a buy-out offer at 40 which then became 70 with the appearance of a new suitor. An original offer made for Pillsbury was also raised significantly. Likewise, NWA had an increase when a new suitor arrived on the scene. Selling on the news can be selling too soon.

However, once a situation appears to stabilize, it is wise to sell out before the top is reached. This can be especially difficult as the price keeps moving up near or above the set price. Many investors hang on thinking they will get out at the first sign of trouble. The problem with this thinking is that sudden drops can occur without warning. Profits can be wiped out in a few minutes.

In conclusion, be aware that buying on the rumor and selling on the news is high speculation and filled with risk of loss. There are essentially two types of rumors, announced and unannounced. Once a rumor has made the news media it could be too late to take advantage of it as the stock has already made its move. The unannounced rumor could be a total fabrication that never occurs. Most sophisticated investors stay away from rumor investing. It would be prudent to look for quality stocks which could become attractive acquisition candidates. If companies are not bought out, the investor is still left with a good quality stock at a reasonable price.

Chapter 11

Sell High—Buy Low

Sell short and buy back at a lower price. Wonderful! An investor can make money in a falling market! This strategy can be profitable in the right situation, however, there are considerations to be aware of in order to protect a short position.

Foremost, the investor should keep in mind that a short position has a limited gain (a stock price can only fall to zero) and has potentially unlimited risk (there is no defined top limit for the price of any stock). Eventually the stock that has been sold short must be bought back to cover the position. Perhaps a verse attributed to Daniel Drew, in the late 1800s states the risk most clearly:

> "He who sells what isn't his'n
> Buys it back or goes to prison"

In most cases the risk is controlled by the margin call for more funds when the stock price is rising. A more serious problem can arise if a buy-out offer unexpectedly appears on a stock that has been sold short.

Another important consideration is that stock must be borrowed in order to be sold short. This insures that there won't be more shares sold short than are in existence. Stock is borrowed from the firm placing the order to sell short. If the stock cannot be located within the firm, it is borrowed from another firm. At times there will be a shortage of stock to be borrowed. If the stock cannot be borrowed, it cannot be sold short.

When a shortage of borrowed stock occurs, those lending the stock can call it back at any time, even before settlement date. If the stock cannot be borrowed elsewhere, it can create a situation where the short position must be closed out, no matter what the current profit or loss. The short seller is notified, though not necessarily before the stock is repurchased.

A final word of caution to the short seller: Stock trades on a stock exchange can only be sold short on an "up tick" or a "zero plus" tick. This can make selling short difficult when a market is falling. The purpose of the up tick rule is to prevent a declining stock from being hammered lower by the short sellers. Over the counter stocks are not bound by this up tick rule.

Chapter 12

The Perfect Hedge Is Short Against the Box

Short "against the box" is a conservative situation. The investor owns (long) 100 shares of IBM and sells (short) 100 shares of IBM. This strategy is often called a "perfect hedge." There is no loss if the stock drops in price. On the other hand, there is no gain if the stock rises in price. For example:

Long 100 IBM at 110 = 11,000
Short 100 IBM at 115 = 11,500

If both positions are closed out, the profit is $500.00. If the stock declines, the profit stays the same. If the stock price increases, the profit continues to be $500.00.

Short against the box can be closed by selling the long position and buying back the short position, or the short stock position can be closed by delivering the long stock against the short. Delivering stock to close the short might require a letter of instruction to the broker. No orders are written on delivering, therefore generally no commission is charged.

The perfect hedge can be useful in a situation where the investor currently owns the stock but does not have physical possession. This strategy can benefit the investor who is receiving stock from a corporate purchase plan, but will not receive the certificate for a few days or weeks. Margin requirements must be fulfilled (Regulation T, which currently requires a deposit of 50 percent and all margin maintenance calls must be met if the stock continues to rise in price), but the strategy does lock in the price with the short sell. When the investor receives the stock it can be delivered to close out the short position.

Short selling can be a helpful and profitable strategy in the proper situation, but it should be used with caution. The short seller must be aware of the rules and the risks. The "perfect hedge" short sell can be a useful tool in the right situation, but is limited in terms of additional gain.

Chapter 13
Never Short a Dull Market

A dull market is a sideways market, with little advance or gain. A dull market has an inherent underlying strength, which can turn into a strong rally at a little good news. During most dull or balanced markets the institutional investors are all waiting for a good reason to get back into the market. The slightest good news (or even bad news that is better than expected) can cause a strong rally to develop. The rally can cause the price of the short stock to rise sharply, resulting in margin calls and eventually a loss. The proof of the market strength is shown by the stability creating the dullness. If there was no strength, the market would be falling.

All lethargic markets have the occasional rallies and corrections. The up and down swings of the prices are usually not severe. If one notices where the heaviest volume occurs, it is possible to determine whether the sentiment is bullish or bearish. If the volume on a down correction is consistently and significantly higher than the volume on a rally, the trend is bearish. If, however, the heavier volume appears on the occasional rally, the sentiment is bullish.

1988 was a year with a dull, lethargic market that tended to have rather heavy volume on rallies and lighter volume on corrections. Often the rally action was caused by "dividend capture," the buying of a stock just for the purpose of receiving the dividend.

"Never short a dull market" refers to the underlying strength of stock prices in a market that has become lethargic.

The underlying strength can turn to buying activity on the slightest positive news. The ensuing rally can be difficult for the short position.

Chapter 14

Never Short the Trend

Shorting the trend refers to sell short when a new high is reached in the stock market, or, in an individual stock, when the trend has been definitely upward. The investor is making a large gamble that the market will turn and decline.

The market and the stock might turn or not turn. The fact is stocks tend to move as a group, and trends tend to continue until they make a significant turn and begin a trend in the opposite direction. It can be futile and costly to attempt to short a stock at the "top." This top might be the beginning of a takeover attempt which could be disastrous to a short position.

Often, the best time to short is soon after a significant turn in the market or, after an individual stock experiences bad news.

Cray Research stock, which had been trading above 70 dollars a share in October of 1988, continued to fall on a roller coaster ride to just over 40 dollars a share nearly a year later—a loss that amounted to more than 40 percent in eleven months. This news, of course, continued to drive investors from the stock.

Selling a short position toward the end of June would have been a strategy in line with the current trend. This could have been near the 50 dollar a share level. The short position would have been profitable through November even though there was an earnings improvement in September. Buying back the short position in November could have been at the 32 dol-

Price Movement Chart: Cray Research

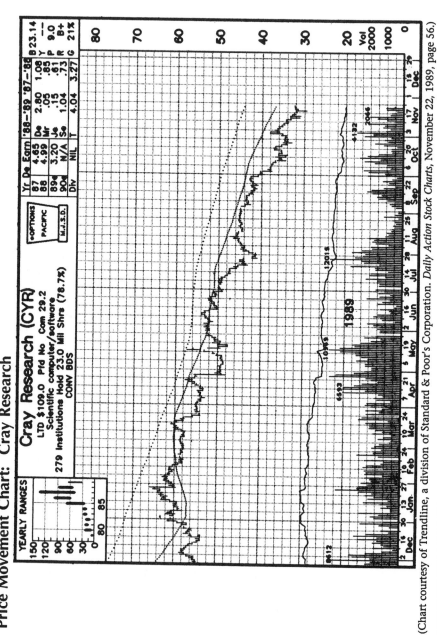

(Chart courtesy of Trendline, a division of Standard & Poor's Corporation. *Daily Action Stock Charts*, November 22, 1989, page 56.)

lar level. A per share profit of 18 dollars a share is attractive. A caution to keep in mind with a stock like this is the nature of its product.

Cray Research is a manufacturer of supercomputers, which are superexpensive and superprofitable. A new sale of just one system could dramatically improve the earnings picture and rally the stock. There is indeed a bottom price for Cray Research in this decline, but it is difficult with the information in hand to know where that price will be. Because of this, most short sellers will close a short position by buying back the stock when they have achieved a profit objective. They won't even try to hit the bottom.

The bad news at Cray began with lowered earnings estimates and layoffs; it continued when the company founder left to form an entirely new corporation. A bad news situation can be quite attractive if there is a potential for even more bad news. The short sell strategy can be used effectively in a number of ways, but it is important to understand the mechanics, rules and risks involved.

Chapter 15

Never Buy a Stock Because It Has a Low Price

Buying a stock just because the price is low is often a risky strategy, however, there are situations where a lower price can be *one* of the selection factors.

The term *"oversold"* can refer to a technical condition with an individual stock, or it can refer to a situation which causes a stock to drop lower in price due to the release of information regarding the earnings potential of a company. Actually the stock becomes "undervalued," meaning that the price is lower than the current value based on current earnings.

When a company which has been established with consistent earnings over several years comes out with negative information, the price will likely drop.

If we take a look at a price chart for Toys "R" Us, a number of interesting facts become apparent.

The price chart shows a certain amount of price lethargy from January through March, with a relatively strong surge toward the end of April. This was related to the upcoming three-for-two split that occurred at the end of May. Earnings through April did not show a great deal of strength. Fourteen cents per share vs. 11 cents per share. At this point the split was not being aided by the earnings. A small selloff in May tested the strength of the stock. With no further positive news forthcoming, a stronger selloff in June caused the stock to fall below 28 dollars a share. This point could be called an "oversold" or "undervalued" situation.

Price Movement Chart: Toys "R" Us

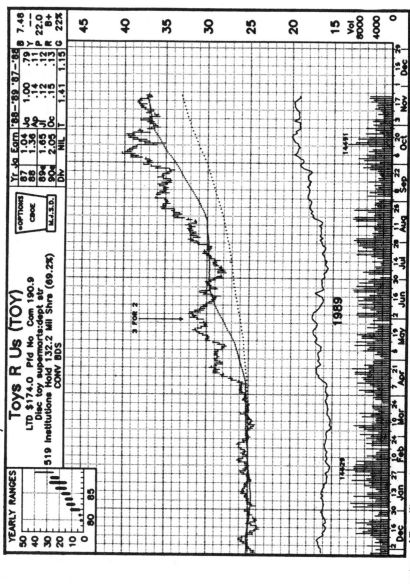

(Chart courtesy of Trendline, a division of Standard & Poor's Corporation. *Daily Action Stock Charts*, November 22, 1989, page 173.)

Note that this was the third time in four months that the stock was selling at this level. The last such occurrence, in May, led to a significant rally. Even though July earnings (12 cents vs. 12 cents for the previous year's same quarter) did not show a significant increase, they did not show a decline either.

Toys "R" Us began a significant rally to the 37 dollar level. The price/earnings ratio at this point was 22. This would be considered high by many investors, but if we look at the P/E history it is about average.

We see that the P/E ratio runs in a range between 18 and 25 for the past five years. A P/E of 22, though somewhat above the 1988 level of 18 is not way out of line.

An "oversold" or "undervalued" situation can be an ideal time to buy any stock, but it is important to know more than just the price of the stock and its current P/E ratio.

At times a drop in the stock price brings even more sellers to the market, which causes the price to drop even further. Many times the selling momentum will force the price lower than the implications of the bad news. This can create a temporary oversold situation. The difficulty lies in determining two factors: Is all of the bad news out and has too much damage been done?

Will the bad news of lower earnings lead to more bad news of employee layoffs and further restricted production capabilities? Have the institutional traders dumped their positions in the stock and moved somewhere else?

Eastman Kodak stock has experienced various bouts with bad news since 1986, when they lost a crucial court battle on patent rights to the competition Poloroid Corporation. After significant expense in research and development, Eastman Kodak dropped out of the instant camera market, a billion dollar a year market. Earnings suffered for the remainder of 1986 and again in 1987. In January of 1988 Kodak bought Sterling Drug, Inc. for just over five billion dollars. This allowed them to enter the pharmaceutical business.

Price Movement Chart: Eastman Kodak

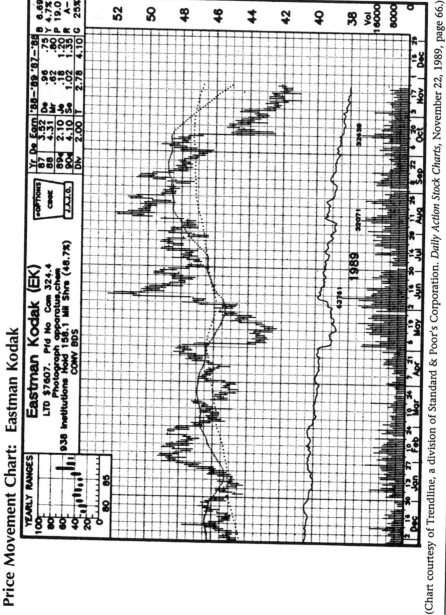

(Chart courtesy of Trendline, a division of Standard & Poor's Corporation. *Daily Action Stock Charts*, November 22, 1989, page 66.)

Still, the news for Eastman Kodak grew worse. In May of 1989, the first quarter net dropped 23 percent to 62 cents a share. In August of 1989 an 85 percent drop in the second quarter net to 18 cents a share (which included a $227 million restructuring charge) added greatly to the volatility of the stock.

It is easy to see how the bad news in May of 1989 caused the stock to decline sharply. Also obvious is the high level of volatility developing in the stock. The volatility is partly caused by a continuation of the negative news emerging and is also caused by the emergence of buyers. The presence of these buyers suggests that a significant number of investors believes that Eastman Kodak will be able to weather this storm. Volatility also suggests that all the bad news might not yet be known.

If the company is fundamentally sound, with a good product and is likely to regain the market share within the next year or so, the stock price will probably recover quickly. This is particularly true of a company that has an earnings loss due to problems with a new product or new market and still has steady income from their regular, well-established line.

If the company is rather new or has a narrow product range being threatened, the damage can be severe and it can be long-term damage to the price. It might even become permanent and put the company out of business. Remember Coleco, and the cute little dolls so many parents could not live without?

Determining whether or not all of the bad news is out is difficult. Some types of news seem to suggest that more problems will follow while other types of bad news are isolated and unique. Problems with a new product or new market can lead to further difficulties in sales and growth. These problems can go either way. The main line earnings might be sufficient to continue the growth of the company or they could be hindered by the losses with the new product line (such as with Eastman Kodak's instant camera experiences).

An industrial accident, such as an oil spill or damaging facility incident, while unfortunate, might have a temporary or insignificant impact on earnings. EXXON had a severe oil spill in 1989 that had little effect on the price of the stock. It could have had some effect on the price growth, but did not drive the price much lower. When the price did drop, it recovered within just a few days. Insurance and tax benefits helped maintain earnings and price in this situation.

Plant layoffs or closings can go either way. They might cut expenses therefore improve earnings or they might be a sign of increasing problems. This is often the time to look for more bad news. Fundamental balance sheet analysis can be helpful in determining the benefits of closings.

A fundamental knowledge of the company whose stock has fallen can be most helpful in determining whether or not a price recovery is apt to be slow or rapid. If the chances of a price recovery are good, the price will often begin to recover quickly, although it will usually not recover fully for some time. Full price recovery will usually need time for the growth in earnings to improve.

A sharp correction in the stock market can also cause an oversold situation with individual stocks. The profits of an individual company can remain strong while the entire market has dropped, pulling all of the stocks to lower prices. Once the market appears to have stabilized, the investor should look for those companies that remain strong on earnings. This can be an excellent buying opportunity. The market crash of 1987 created several bargains at low prices.

Buying oversold stocks is a strategy used by many investors in which they buy recently depressed stocks with which they are familiar. The key is to buy the stock in relation to its earnings, rather than buying stock because it has a low price. Many stocks with low prices are actually expensive in relation to earnings. Investors buying oversold stocks might have a short-term gain objective and an alternate long-term objective if the stock takes a longer time to recover. This can be an effective strategy in a bull market, but can be very disappointing in a bearish market, where downward market pressure is contributing to a lowering of prices.

Chapter 16

Beware the "Penny Stock"

"Penny stocks" have some interesting characteristics: the price per share is low, the price will usually go lower and the risk is exceptionally high.

There are several different definitions of "penny stock." Some investors define a penny stock as any stock with a price of less than ten dollars, five dollars, three dollars, two dollars, or one dollar. If a stock is issued originally as a penny stock, in many cases, the company itself did the underwriting. There were several million shares issued and the stock is not "blue sky" (approved for trading) in every state.

These conditions can make trading the stock difficult or, at times, altogether impossible. The liquidity is more than adequate in terms of shares an investor can buy, but there are not always enough buyers when the investor wants to sell out and take the loss.

The amount of risk in the low price situation increases dramatically as the price of the stock drops lower. It can be true that reward potential increases as risk increases, but this is not necessarily true in a penny stock.

If a company whose stock is selling for about fifty cents has two or three employees left (who are looking for work) and they are unable to manufacture product or even ship product, that company will most likely go out of business and the stock will drop to zero.

Some investors are attracted to stocks like these. The usual statement made is "I thought I'd invest a thousand dollars and if I lose it okay, but I might get lucky." In the vast majority of cases, they don't get lucky and the thousand dollars is gone. The odds are probably better in horse racing or in a trip to Las Vegas where they at least get some entertainment for their money.

Another problem encountered with very low-priced stocks is the cost of commissions. Charges can run as much as 30 to 50 percent or more (they are allowed to be as high as 80 percent). Brokerage firms charge more of a percentage for these stocks, but not necessarily more dollars. The same commission might be charged for an identical amount of a higher priced stock. Some penny stock can be purchased directly from a company, but the company might not be willing to buy the stock back.

Unless the investor wants to own and manage the company, the super low-priced penny stocks are usually best avoided. These stocks have had a lot of bad press and legal actions in the past couple of years and are already being avoided by the majority of investors.

If an investor feels an overwhelming urge to invest in the low-priced stocks, it is a good idea to choose those for which the brokerage firm has research information available. This will at least give some information as to the company's prospects for recovery.

Chapter 17

Give Stop Orders "Wiggle" Room

A *stop order* is an order to buy or sell stock, once a predetermined price is traded at or through. Buy stop orders are placed above the current trading price and sell stop orders are placed below the current price. Once activated, the order becomes a "market order," which says the investor wants to receive the best available price.

Wiggle room is important when placing stop orders—whether one is buying or selling stock. Essentially, it allows the stock price to move in "normal" market swings without activating the stop. Wiggle room is placing the stop close enough to the current price to prevent a loss on a sell or activate a buy on an upward move, but far enough from the current price that it will only be activated by a major move.

When buying, the investor wants the "buy stop" to be activated only if the stock price is making a strong move upward. On the other side, no one really wants the "sell stop" order to be filled, unless the market and the stock are declining at a disturbing rate. Consequently, the buy stop is usually placed closer to the current trading range than is the sell stop. It is good to give the sell stop enough room for the price to fall and recover without having the stop activate.

Placing the buy stop order requires some study of the current trading range. The distance between the buy stop price and the current trading price of the stock is a matter of personal preference, based on trading range analysis. Looking at a price chart is the best way to calculate where to place the buy stop order. It doesn't really do any harm to place the order too high, as the investor can change the order and bring it lower if necessary.[1]

Take a look at the following graph for Tyco Laboratories. An investor following Tyco observed the move in December, on good earnings, followed by another step up in February, again with earnings growth. This earnings growth and a history showing a 22 percent growth rate for the past five years make this stock a good candidate for investment. An investor could make further analysis or could decide to buy the stock as it moves.

In the second week of April, 1989, the stock began to show weakness as the price drifted lower. Price weakness in a quality stock should be looked at as a potential buying opportunity. Once an investor believes the stock to be stable (not dropping further) and yet still a growth opportunity, it is time to take action.

Tyco was trading between 34 and 35 dollars a share. It had been up to nearly 38 dollars and down to almost 33 dollars a share, a five dollar per share swing. The decision was made to buy 500 shares of Tyco with a buy stop order. This strategy was used because the investor does not know when the price will recover. Indeed, more bad news might emerge and the stock could drift lower. Like Will Rogers advised, the investor only wants to buy the stock if it goes up. Extra money will be paid for this strategy, but if the move is correct, the profits will more than cover the extra cost.

---

1   Stop orders and stop loss orders are now being accepted by some firms for over the counter (OTC) stocks on an experimental basis. In most cases stop orders will only be accepted for stocks trading on the exchanges and not for OTC stocks.

Price Movement Chart: Tyco Laboratories

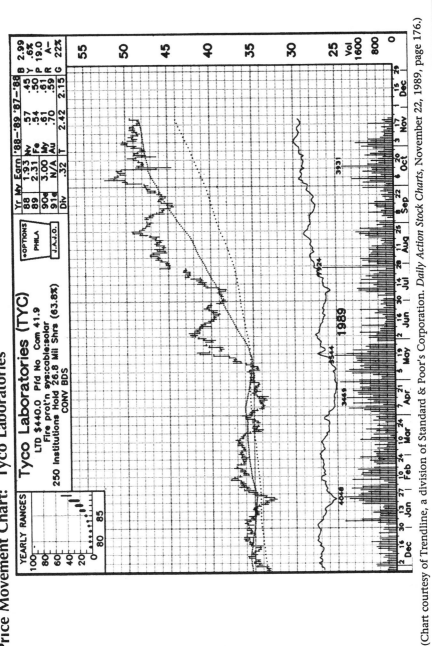

(Chart courtesy of Trendline, a division of Standard & Poor's Corporation. *Daily Action Stock Charts*, November 22, 1989, page 176.)

The main resistance in this short time period (since December) had been at 37 dollars, with one brief run at 38 dollars a share. The investor decided that it would take extraordinary buying strength to break through the resistance. This kind of extraordinary buying would likely carry the stock even higher, partly because it is a high quality stock that moves in surges and also because it is a popular stock with the institutions (250 institutions hold 63.8 percent).[2]

The investor decided to place the buy stop order at 38 dollars a share with a limit of 40 for protection.

BUY: 500 shares of TYC at 38 STOP 40 LIMIT GTC.[3]

The order was not activated during the rest of April. However, during the third week of May the price began to run up. The stop order would have been activated as the price of the trading stock traded at or through the stop price of 38 dollars a share. It most likely would have filled below the limit of 40 dollars. For purposes of this exercise, we will say that the stock was purchased at 39 dollars a share. The position now looked like the following example.

Bought: 500 shares TYC at $39.00 per share.
Total cost = $19,500.00[4]

The investor now owns a stock which is trading nearly five dollars higher than when the order was placed. This strategy has cost an extra premium of $2,500.00.

The premium of extra cost is created by placing the buy order above the current market price. Some would add this premium on to the actual cost in order to figure a break-even price. For this example we will use actual figures without the extra cost of the premium:

---

2   Actual institutional ownership figures only slightly different for April.
3   GTC: means "good till cancelled."
4   The example does not take commissions into account.

Total stock cost = $19,500.00.
Divided by 500
Total Cost per share = 39 dollars

This is the break-even price for the investor. The price at which the profits begin.[5]

At this point, many conservative investors will place a *sell stop* order (also called a stop loss). Many aggressive investors prefer to wait with this order until there is some profit to protect. If the profit fails to develop, they will sell quickly and move on to the next strategy.

For the following example we will place a stop sell order. It would be an acceptable strategy to place the sell stop at a basic two dollars away from the buy (37 dollars) or to use a percent such as 8 or 10 percent below the purchase price of 39 dollars.

A distance of 10 percent would be a stop price at 35 dollars. If the stock drops and the sell stop is activated at 35 dollars a share, the results would look something like this:

SOLD:

500 shares at $35.00 per share =	$17,500.00
Total Cost Purchase	$19,500.00
Sell Proceeds	$17,500.00
Total Loss	$ 2,000.00

A loss of 2,000 dollars is not a wonderful thought, but can be more acceptable than say a 50 percent loss. Keeping in mind that the preference is not to activate a sell stop order, let us look at another possible strategy.

Again we look at the price graph. There is fairly good support at the 34 dollar range. On one occasion the price broke down through 34 dollars and approached the 33 dollar level. One could reasonably believe that it would take a truly major correction to break through that 33 dollar level. If such

---

5   The actual break-even price will be higher due to commission costs.

a correction occurred, the price would likely keep dropping. This could also be a level for a stop loss price.

SELL: 500 TYC at 33 STOP GTC.

Say the dreaded correction does happen, and the stock drops far enough to activate the 33 dollar sell stop price:

SOLD:
500 TYC at 33 = $16,500
Total Cost Purchase $19,500 (with premium)
Proceeds from Sell $16,500
Total Loss $ 3,000

There are essentially two arguments favoring the lower sell stop price.

- The investor has more time to step in and change the order, if necessary, before the stop is activated. Obviously, the loss would not be as great.
- The sell stop is less likely to be activated by a minor market swing. Its purpose is to protect as much as possible of the original investment while the investor is unable to keep an eye on things. (Few people have the luxury of watching their stocks every trading hour.)

July would have been a difficult time for this investor. The stock price rose through the 40 dollar break-even point, went up to 42 1/2 and began to drop. Granted a 1,250 dollar profit in a couple of months would have been good, but the stock did not stay at that level for long. May earnings were flat (61 cents vs. 61 cents per share), but the lead from the first of the year remained in force. Earnings were again strong in August (70 cents vs. 59 cents).

Rather than take the profit, one strategy might be to begin raising the sell stop price. It would have been possible to raise the stop into profitable territory and still keep it from being executed. Sell stop at 43 or even 44 would have been safe.

The sell stop can be useful protection in any situation where a profit is involved. It can also be used to control some of the loss in a severe decline. It is important to remember to place stop orders far enough away from the current price so that they are not activated by minor price swings. The buy stop can be placed closer as it is an order that investors prefer to have filled. Price protection can be added by also placing a limit on the buy stop. The sell stop needs a bit more room as the preference is that it not be filled. A price limit can also be used if one keeps in mind that it might prevent the order from being executed. The orders are best used where they demand significant movement in prices. If the investor feels the urge to place a stop order close to the current price, it might be better to simply place a market order and save the extra dollars.

Chapter 18

Buy the Stock That Splits

"This stock split two for one at 40 dollars a share and ran up to 40 again within a six-month period. It's just incredible how fast this company is growing. The stock is now at 42 dollars a share and there is talk of another two for one split! It would be great to have more stocks like this one . . ."

This is obviously the sound of a happy investor. Stock splits are good news and the price will often continue to increase, given time. Even though this is often the case it is not always what happens; the price does not have to increase and not all stock splits end up being positive.

Every so often the positive stock split story is heard. It might be at a cocktail party or a business lunch. Such a story will invariably hold the attention of the listeners. Many sincerely wish they had bought the stock a year ago, when the price was more reasonable. Now observe in the chart on the following page what a stock split can do to the price of a stock. At Shaw Industries, a two for one stock split occurred in the first part of May, with the stock trading just over 36 dollars a share.

The split caused the stock to trade just over 18 dollars a share. For the next month the stock drifts lower. This is most likely due to the run-up caused by the announcement of the split. Positive earnings at the end of June and again in September continued to bring buyers to the stock. By the first part of November the stock was again trading above 30 dollars a share. This is a gain of 12 dollars from the split at 18. This is more than a 66 percent gain on the stock in less than six months. It is no wonder we see some profit taking in November.

Price Movement Chart: Shaw Industries

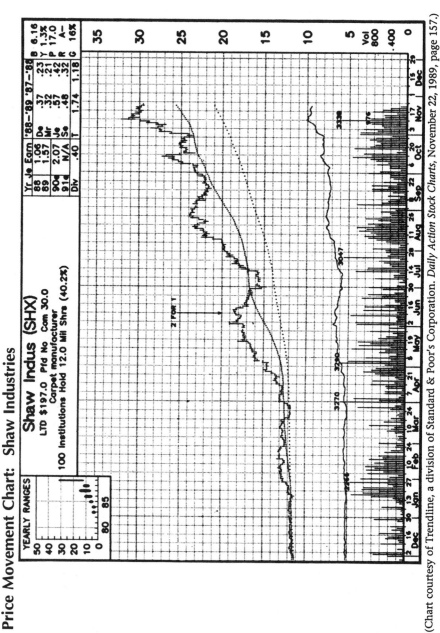

(Chart courtesy of Trendline, a division of Standard & Poor's Corporation. *Daily Action Stock Charts*, November 22, 1989, page 157.)

The most common stock splits are also known as forward splits and are often described as stock dividends.

Stock splits:

2 for 1
3 for 1
3 for 2

These are common split quantities and are usually good news. The splits increase the number of shares outstanding, thereby increasing the liquidity (the amount of stock available for buying and selling) of the stock and they lower the price per share of the stock.

The lowering of the price makes the stock more affordable to investors. The price of the split stock, as well as all the other per share financial data, is lowered in a proportionate amount to the new added shares.

For example: A stock selling at $50.00 splits two for one. The end result is twice as many shares of a stock now selling at $25.00 per share.

The prices of recently split stocks will often rise in a relatively short period of time. This is particularly true of stocks that continue to have positive news emerging. New contracts, increased sales or improved earnings are helpful in pushing up the price of such a stock. An investor can make some good market moves by investing in stocks that have had recent splits.

The question arises as to whether it is generally better to buy the stock before or after the split occurs. This can be more difficult to ascertain than one might imagine. The price of the stock might rise on the announcement and continue to rise after the split actually takes place. However, if the reason for the split was to give support to a weakening stock (it happens), the price will likely drop after the split occurs. It is safe to say that the decision to buy a stock before or after a split should not be based solely on the split, but rather on earnings and earnings anticipation.

One positive reason to buy before the split relates to the cost of commission. Commission prices are usually based on quantity and price. If the stock is purchased before a two for one split the commission will likely be significantly lower.

As always, there is some risk involved with stock splits: the stock might decline after a split or unexpected bad news could cause a severe drop in price. If there are twice as many shares, bad news can have a considerably stronger effect.

An additional risk is that the investor could miss out on the split. Splits have an "EX" date, just like cash dividends. Buying on or after the "EX" date does not qualify an investor for the split. However, the stock will be purchased at the lower adjusted post split price.

Another factor to consider is that options trade differently after a split. They can trade as a totally different kind of option. For example, what happens if an investor has one option contract (for 100 shares) and the stock splits three for two. Does the investor now have one contract for 100 shares and another contract for 50 shares or does the investor have one contract for 150 shares, or is the strike price of the option changed to reflect the split? How does the investor calculate the time value and the inherent premium value of the new option? What happens to the strike price of the new option?

All of this confusion can have an effect on the price of a stock involved with a split. Many investors simply close out their positions and move on to something less complicated.

Considered by many investors to be the most negative aspect of a split stock is the time involved for the new (when issued shares) to be delivered. Many professional traders just don't like the idea of tying up assets and waiting for the delivery of new shares, even though it might take only a few days.

Although stock splits are generally viewed as a positive event, the price does not automatically increase just because of the split. Here is an example where the price declined significantly after a stock split.

Note that the stock ran up before the split actually occurred, but then headed south after the event. September earnings didn't help the situation.

Now look at a stock which had two splits in one year.

Price Movement Chart: Computer Associates Intl.

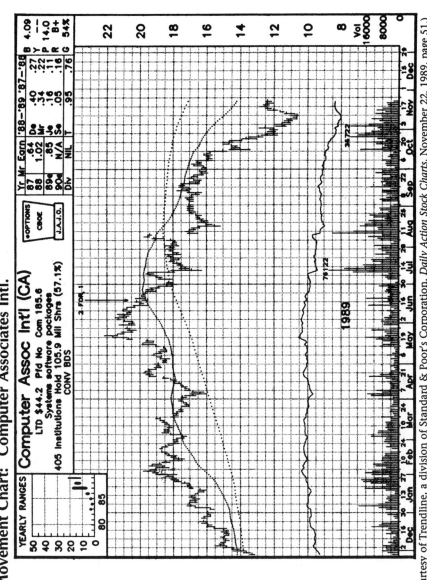

(Chart courtesy of Trendline, a division of Standard & Poor's Corporation. *Daily Action Stock Charts*, November 22, 1989, page 51.)

Quantum appears to have done well after the three for two split, but not so well after the two for one split four months later. It is unusual to see more than one stock split for the same company in less than a one-year period of time. It can be a sign of rapid growth or it can become an over extension. It is not necessarily the split that causes the price to decline, but rather the magnification caused by the split. If some of the institutional holders cut their positions, they are selling considerably more shares than they would have before the splits occurred. It should be mentioned that Quantum Corp. was attaining new highs in mid-May of 1990. This quick recovery from price weakness is often a sign of a strong performer.

Reverse Splits

Reverse splits are consolidations done for only one real purpose—to give support to the stock price by bringing it up where it might be more attractive for trading. They are usually one for 10 or one for 20 and can be even higher. One for 10 means that for every 10 shares investors currently own, they now own only one share. One hundred shares would become 10 shares. The price will temporarily increase tenfold, but will usually begin to fall as investors begin to sell. A reverse split is not looked at as a positive sign. It is often, but not always, a last ditch effort to keep a company alive and trading.

Stock splits are often good news. It is not the split itself that is so important, but rather the performance of earnings behind the stock split. There is no rule that says the price has to increase after a split. Often times the stock will become more volatile and the price will drop. Investors would do well to look at the information behind the split to decide whether to buy, hold or sell.

Price Movement Chart: Quantum Corp.

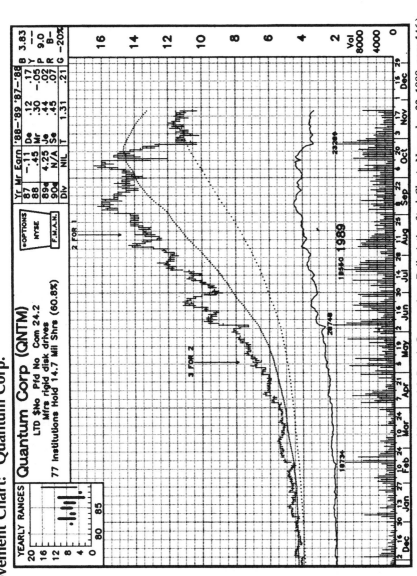

(Chart courtesy of Trendline, a division of Standard & Poor's Corporation. *Daily Action Stock Charts*, November 22, 1989, page 146.)

Chapter 19

Institutions Show Where the Action Is Now

"Any stock in too many institutional portfolios or the subject of excess advisory bullishness should be suspect. Someday a majority will want to take profits."

Gerald M. Loeb

It is an often-stated belief that 20 to 30 percent institutional ownership is an enviable situation. The institutions like it, therefore it must be a good stock! This is basically true; a certain amount of institutional ownership of a stock is a desirable situation. However, like the difficulties encountered by the sorcerer's apprentice when he could not stop the magic, it is possible to have too much of this good thing.

The problem lies in sudden sellouts and profit taking. Stocks with large institutional ownership might have adequate shares for trading in normal, steady markets but this can change rather suddenly. If 40 percent or 50 percent of the stockholders or institutional investors suddenly become sellers, the price can only drop.

Selling of a heavily owned institutional stock can also be triggered in a strong up market. If a company is fundamentally sound and earnings growth is satisfactory and the institutions own 50 to 60 percent of a stock, the stock might not move much during a strong market rally. Volume of the individual stock can be low, showing that no one is selling or buying. The market continues to rally, but the stock just sits in the institution's portfolio. When the rest of the stock market becomes attractive enough, the institutions might decide to pull their dollars out of this stock, which isn't moving, and realign those assets where the action is currently taking place. This can be severe to the price of the one stock.

Some investment analysts claim that the percentage of institutional ownership is not as important as the number of institutions owning the stock. If a hundred or two hundred institutions own 60 percent of one stock this will become a problem if they all begin selling at about the same time. No one can argue with this logic. However, there are two facts which somewhat offset the "too much institutional ownership" debate.:

- It is difficult to find a good stock which is not heavily owned by institutions.

- If the institutions do not like a particular stock, significant price growth is unlikely.

Stocks selected randomly have institutional ownership like the following:

Stock	*# of Institutions*	*% Owned by Institutions* [1]
Reebok Intl.	183	24.9%
Ball Corp.	121	53.6
Archer-Daniels-Mid.	443	53.2
Apple Computer	523	70.4
Ferro Corp.	132	48.7
IBM	1695	49.3
Intel. Corp.	124	67.8
Kemper Corp.	159	49.4
General Mills	515	58.3
Johnson Controls	219	45.6

---

1   Figures as of November, 1989.

These are all good companies in several different industries. Computers, food, insurance, clothing, a wide cross section of business and industry. Yet if one truly followed the idea of avoiding heavily institutionally owned stocks, many of these would be quickly eliminated and that could be a serious investment error.

The fact is many good stocks tend to be heavily owned by institutions. Rather than avoiding stocks with heavy institutional ownership, one should look for its presence and notice any significant changes. In fact, it is also interesting to note that the institutional ownership of many stocks does not change much month to month. Now look at the figures in comparison to three months later.

Stock	# of Institutions			% Owned by Institutions		
	11/89	2/90	+/–	11/89	2/90	+/–
Reebok Intl.	183	185	+2	24.9	26.7	+1.8
Ball Corp.	121	121	0	53.6	52.9	–0.7
Archer-Daniels-Mid.	443	437	–6	53.2	48.5	–4.7
Apple Computer	523	504	–19	70.4	66.3	–4.1
Ferro Corp.	132	111	–21	48.7	44.2	–4.5
IBM	1695	1480	–219	49.3	48.5	–0.8
Intel Corp.	124	121	–3	67.8	67.6	–0.2
Kemper Corp.	159	172	+13	49.4	46.5	–2.9
General Mills	515	507	–8	58.3	61.9	+3.6
Johnson Controls	219	205	–14	45.6	51.5	+5.9

It is easy to see that changes in institutional ownership do occur. IBM dropped 219 institutions, but only .8 percent of ownership. Kemper Corp. gained 13 institutions but fell 2.9 percent in overall institutional ownership. These changes are not particularly dramatic. Followed over several months time, they can show either a significant increase or decrease of institutional interest in any given stock.

But how do price changes compare to these institutional changes? Let's take a look.

Stock	Price 11/89	Price 2/90	Change
Reebok Intl.	17 3/8	18	+5/8
Ball Corp.	30 1/2	30 1/4	–1/4
Archer-Daniels-Mid.	32 1/8	21 (31.5)²	–5/8
Apple Computer	44 1/4	34	–10 1/4
Ferro Corp.	27 1/2	23 1/2	–4
IBM	97 5/8	103 7/8	+6 1/4
Intel Corp.	21 7/8	19 1/4	–2 5/8
Kemper Corp.	47	38 1/8	–8 7/8
General Mills	74 5/8	64 1/4	–10 3/8
Johnson Controls	30 5/8	28 1/4	–2 3/8

It is interesting to note that only IBM and Reebok Intl. were up for the time period and yet change in institutional ownership was down for IBM and up only a small amount for Reebok. The largest price drop was General Mills, down 10 3/8 dollars, and yet the percent of institutional ownership was up 3.6 (although the number of institutional owners dropped by 8).

Even if this analysis were expanded it would likely remain inconclusive. The reason is simple, institutional ownership of stocks is constantly changing. Each owner bought the stock at different prices, and as they gain profits or decide to take losses they sell part or all of their positions. Other institutions then build a position by buying stock.

Heavy institutional ownership does indeed bring the risk of falling prices due to sell off, but it is still more desirable than a lack of institutional ownership.

---

2   3 for 2 stock split in December 1989.

Below are some stocks which are lower in institutional ownership.

1989 Prices

Stock	*# Inst.*	*%*	*High*	*Low*
Wendy's Intl.	131	21.6	4 7/8	3 7/8
Winnebago	41	21.1	5 5/8	4 3/8
Sunshine Mine	63	8.5	4	3 1/4
Pan Am	97	18.5	4	2 1/2
Kit MFG.	12	18.0	6	5 3/8

These could all become excellent companies and could be good growth opportunities. The point is that stocks with low institutional interest tend to have slower growth, and trade in narrow price ranges.

This is not to say that institutional investors are all great geniuses in picking the best stocks. They have many of the same difficulties as the individual investor. The great advantage to the institution is capital resources. They tend to have a virtually inexhaustible supply of money. A bad decision disappears with the next trade.

To some extent, many institutional investors are not concerned with the quality of a stock. They place a certain amount of their portfolio into so-called "quality investments," but the remainder of the assets are used to play a money game of "fishing" for opportunity. At times the game takes on aspects of a "search and destroy" mission. They have the ability to run a stock up only to turn around and hammer it back down. The continued outcry against "programmed trading" is a testimony to the problems caused by the antics of many institutional investors.

Remember the example of "averaging up," where it was possible to buy stock at an average price below the current market value? That's fine with a few thousand dollars, but think of the impact this strategy could have with a few million dollars to invest. It literally could drive the price of a stock upward, drawing in new investors along the way. When a certain level is reached, a sell button is pushed and the stock drops back down to former levels and lower. The losers are the ones left holding the bag. If this sell occurs just before the market closes even, many of the other institutions are left holding the bag.

Is this manipulation? Technically it is not considered actual manipulation, but the effect is the same. Whether a single stock's price is driven up by buying or hammered down by selling, the facts are clear. The stock price is being maneuvered and it doesn't matter what reason is given. The usual published reason is the arbitrage situation between owning the stock or owning the future or index option. This is something akin to children moving their quarrelsome game into the next yard. The action got too unpredictable with the stocks so they switched to the futures for a cooling off period.

This tremendous financial power in the hands of the institutional investor must be at least partly understood by the individual who wishes to be a stock trader. The investor should know when to ride out the volatility and possibly when to count on some price swings; a buying opportunity might suddenly appear. At times it can be like a game of "crack the whip" played on the slippery ice. This is why it can be prudent to place orders with some protective qualifiers (see section on types of orders and order modifiers).

Institutional ownership of a stock can be a consideration, but it is part of the investment game. Changes in ownership might be significant, but this information can be too late to use for advantage. Lack of institutional ownership can be a larger concern for the individual investor.

Chapter 20

Avoid Heavy Positions in Thinly Traded Stocks

Two concepts in the statement above are often more subjective than objective. "Heavy" and "thinly," can be determined differently by investors. A heavy position for one might be five to ten thousand shares, for another it could mean a few hundred shares. Thinly traded might be a stock which doesn't trade on some days, or it could mean a stock which trades less than 5,000 shares a day. The terms are not absolute, however, the two terms should be considered together as heavy position and thinly traded.

A heavy position of a thinly traded stock is one which cannot be easily and quickly sold. This might be several thousand shares or it can be a couple of hundred shares. It depends on the average daily trading volume, which can be learned by observation or research. Many stock traders would consider anything less than 10,000 shares a day as thin.

Thinly traded stocks also tend to have relatively low prices, often below three dollars a share. A problem can arise in this way: although it is relatively easy to buy 10,000 shares of a thinly traded stock, it could be difficult to sell the position. Selling might necessitate breaking the block into smaller segments of 5,000 or 3,000 or even 1,000 shares. All of those shares "hitting the bid" (pushing the price lower by selling) can be damaging to profits and helpful in increasing losses. The investor can also be charged additional commissions if the transactions, buys or sells cannot be executed on the same day.

Thinly traded stocks might be worth a light speculative position of a few hundred shares held for a long-term investment. But they should probably not make up a significant position for short-term trading.

Chapter 21

There Are At Least Two Sides to a Story

Like a monster with two formidable heads, the news presents two sides to a story: one with prosperity and riches, the other with doom and gloom. The news media appears to have considered the stock market unpredictable for some time. Rather than take sides, the news media often takes a more political route, in the middle. If a story is told in two opposing ways, the believer will take the version most associated with his or her understanding. This is basic human nature. We tend to believe what we want to believe. The individual claims that beliefs are based on logic and reasoning, but the fact is beliefs tend to be founded in a good deal of emotion.

If one listens carefully to the message of the media, whether television or the newspapers, when it comes to finance there are nearly always two opposing viewpoints presented. Then in the future at least one of the two points is likely to be correct.

There is even a more basic reason for this duplicity. No one is able to foretell the future. If the news media presented one side of a belief without the other they would be guilty of attempting to predict something. This would no longer be news, since news is the reporting of what has happened. The news media would prefer not to be remembered for predicting some event which fails to occur, and this is why a double story is told.

There is also a nobler reason. The news media tries to present the facts to both sides of the story and let the consumer decide which "truth" works best for him. The important information is found in the basic facts of economic indicators, political policies and interest rates. Business trends, stock market data and other factual pieces of information add to the picture. Understanding and interpreting these facts and events can easily lead to differences of opinion. Although the news media enjoys pointing out opinion differences, the preference is to remain rather neutral.

The most usable news and information is that which is the most recent. News programs throughout the day keep us updated on political and economic events. It is safe to say that the market is reacting accordingly, whether the news is positive or negative. In most but not all cases the news at the end of a given day is old news. The market has already made its adjustment.

The stock traders, whether professional trader or individual investor, have been watching as the stories developed. In many cases this fresh news was a material influence on their trading decisions. This can be a cause of continual frustration to the individual investor who does not have the immediate access to news as it happens. This is one more reason to make careful trading decisions and take protective actions where necessary.

Chapter 22

Follow a Few Stocks Well

"It is easier to follow a few stocks well than it is to follow a well full of stocks."

S. A. Nelson

Following stocks can be interesting and exciting or it can be tedious and frustrating. To many investors it is the information that starts their day. They thrill to poring over *The Wall Street Journal* or *Barron's* or *Investors' Daily* and other financial journals. Some of these fastidious readers never invest in the stock market. They just enjoy the game, much like watching the World Series or perhaps the Super Bowl. They are the armchair investors who often get a great deal of enjoyment in seeing how the game plays out. This is fine, for entertainment, but it is not generally as interesting as the real experience.

To truly learn skills in stock watching or tracking, one must have firsthand experience. An investor will learn more owning a stock for two weeks than in watching a stock for two years. The reason is simple. Ownership which places ones money at risk greatly heightens the attention. The losses, as the price drops lower, are real losses. More importantly, the gains also become real. The investor's attention is drawn like a magnet to any news about their stock. In the first few days of ownership, most investors will learn more about their companies' stock than they will learn during the remaining holding period. Keeping some of this enthusiasm can prove useful in making sound investment decisions.

There are essentially three main influences on the price of any particular stock: the direction and strength of the stock market, the current "play," or theme, of the stock and earnings.

The direction and strength of the stock market can be difficult to pinpoint, but is usually fairly obvious to anyone reading the most basic market information and opinions. More information is available on determining market strength or weakness throughout this book.

The "play," or theme, of a particular stock is the sector of industry to which the companies' business relates. These might be obvious in cases such as computers, oil, steel, health care or waste management. Others can be more illusive, such as fiber optics, drug rehabilitation or lasers. The potential of lasers has excited people for more than 25 years and yet few companies have accomplished much as "laser companies."

There are also companies that have sought to diversify into many different industries and have become conglomerates, such as the tobacco industries moving more into food products. Sometimes this makes for a stronger company and sometimes it makes a lethargic slow-moving stock that moves slowly in another market.

The importance of classifying a stock by theme or play is simple. It helps to focus the attention on information which will help that particular industry sector and hopefully a particular stock. If OPEC is fighting and producing more oil than usual, the market is soon flooded and oil company stock prices fall in the expectations of lower earnings. However, if the oil producing companies are in a cooperative mood and earnings are on the increase, stock prices will also likely increase.

If the politicians are talking themes of cleaning up the environment and are not interested in building a space platform, it might be a better move to invest in clean-up companies rather than stocks of companies which rely heavily on aerospace spending.

Another important reason to follow the play or theme of individual stocks is the great influence of institutional investors. They tend to spend a great deal of time and money trying to anticipate shifts in popularity among the various industry sectors.

Even many technical traders, who focus tightly on market trends and stock price movement trends will concede the importance of earnings. The trick is to trade not so much on earnings as on the anticipation of earnings. It is often the increase in earnings that will make the stock price rise. Buyers are attracted to the positive news and the stock quickly moves up to higher levels. Many investors who buy at this point are actually buying the stock at inflated prices. When the reality of this becomes evident, the stock retreats. A small profit can quickly become a disappointing loss. This can be especially true of stocks which show a sudden increase in earnings.

Take a look at a price chart for GTE Corp. Notice the earnings improvement that appears just before significant price increases.

Earnings which are showing an increasing trend can be a particularly interesting situation. This can be further enhanced by a company that is in an industry sector with growing importance. The best example would be the progress of many computer stocks over the past 15 to 20 years.

More recently, the conditions favoring the overcrowded airline industry caused some stocks to have exciting earnings and exciting moves. Airline deregulation, as a play, didn't necessarily make flying better but the move did favor the stocks of many aggressive carriers. Earnings *are* important to how a stock trades.

Price earnings ratios can be helpful to a point, but they can be distorted by various factors. Many people who follow such ratios often fail to go a step further than the P/E ratio itself. They will say a price earnings ratio is high because it is above 14 or low because it is below 9. They might even compare the P/E ratio to the average of the Dow Jones Industrial Average. But the full usefulness of the P/E ratio is often overlooked.

Price Movement Chart: GTE Corp.

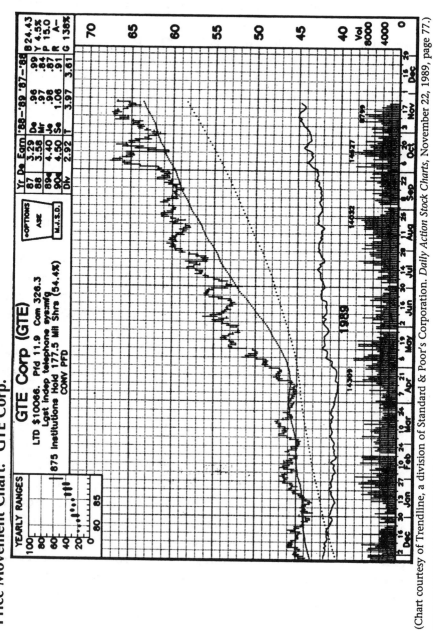

How does the current P/E ratio compare to previous levels? Is it higher or lower? Why is it higher or lower? Is the company moving into exciting new areas with a lot of new earnings potential? Have earnings been stagnant or on a down cycle driving the ratio lower?

If we look at a company like Liz Claiborne and see that it is trading at a P/E ratio of 11, do we say that's about average to all the rest of the stocks?

Liz Claiborne P/E History

		Price	
Year	P/E	High	Low
1983	13.1	4.7	2.0
1984	10.0	6.6	3.1
1985	14.2	12.4	5.9
1986	19.7	24.3	11.9
1987	21.2	39.1	12.3
1988	12.9	20.0	12.8
1989	12.6	27.5	16.5
	14.8 Average P/E		

A current price/earnings ratio of 11 with the annual average being 14.8 makes Liz Claiborne look quite attractive as a candidate for investment. This is a way to look at a P/E ratio in a useful manner.

How does the P/E ratio of a particular company relate to other P/E ratios within the same basic industry? Is it nearly the same or is it quite different? If there is a difference, what is the reason for the higher or lower P/E?

Liz Claiborne's relative P/E ratio was 1.1, meaning that it was very near the average of the industry. 1.0 would be equal. This again is a positive sign. This analysis does not mean the price of the stock will soon climb, there are other market and economic factors, it just gives some practical meaning to the use of P/E ratios in analysis.[1]

The tracking of a stock price can be useful up to a point, but tracking the influences on that price can be more meaningful. The earnings, the relationship between earnings and price and the comparison to other stocks in the same industry all bring up many questions about stock selection. Finding the answers to these few questions can be the beginning of a firm foundation of stock analysis and reason for tracking.

Stock tracking can be done by hand (i.e., making graphs and comparative tables) or it can be done by research of various stock data publications or it can be done most easily and completely by computer.

---

[1]   Liz Claiborne was also the subject of insider's selling in September of 1989 (see page 35). This may account for the price weakness which also helped to lower the P/E ratio.

Chapter 23

Be Wary of Stock Ideas from a Neighbor

S. A. Nelson, author of the first book on The Dow Theory, (published in the early 1900s)[1] mentions this phenomena. Charles Dow, 1900, also commented on the tendency of individuals to invest in a wildly speculative stock, taking much more risk than they would with their own businesses. Even today it is probable that every stockbroker has heard an investor admit interest in a speculative issue of stock because "a neighbor told them about it." These stock recommendations can come with the best intentions, but they should be looked at with some reservations.

The idea might be a good tip or it might have *been* a good tip. Truly good stock ideas usually don't wait around for the investors to make their moves. By the time the friend or neighbor has spread the word, it could be too late to take any action. Learning more about the tip is a good strategy. Even though timing is often of the essence, answering a few questions can help to prevent a costly mistake. Where did the idea originate? Could it be a rumor? Did a broker recommend the stock? Did the idea appear in a financial journal?

Sometimes a tip can quickly be traced to a reliable source, other times the source is more illusive. The frustrating

---

1   *The ABC of Stock Speculation*, first published in 1903, by S. A. Nelson.

fact is the greater the reliability of the source, the less time there is to take action. If the rumor was discussed in *The Wall Street Journal* or *Investor's Daily* or *The New York Times*, the action has probably already occurred.

Although there are times when the action just gets going as a rumor is discussed. If the closest source is a fellow worker, a friendly conversation might shed some valuable light on the insight. Was the source vision, dream, wishful thinking or from yet another source. Spending some time to ask can save money.

It is also important to find out the nature of the tip: How speculative is the tip? Is it short-term oriented? (a buyout rumor; by whom?) Is it more long term (an acquisition; earnings surprise)? Is it a low-priced stock (less than three dollars)? Is the stock marginable?

Buyout rumors have a way of suddenly appearing and disappearing. Sometimes they are based on sound information and other times they are pure fabrication. The truth sounds as good as the falsehood, and the stock can rise just the same. There are also rumors which turn into announcements, only to run into a stone wall. UAL Corp. became an announcement in 1989 and was unable to obtain financing in October. The stock fell and the market fell.

The old Wall Street saying which says, "Buy on the rumor, sell on the news" appears again. To which one might add "but leave some money on the table." (See Chapter 7). It is highly speculative and subject to great risk. Some positive rumors actually cause a decline in the stock price.

In 1990, Pan Am was subject to rumor. A two to three dollar stock for a year, it handily ran above four when delighted sellers pounded it back down. After about the third rumor, it began to actually lose ground as a new "buyout" entered the rumor mill. This was probably because of an "overhead supply" of sellers with limit sells just above the trading range. As the stock ran up in price, these limit sells would be activated, driving the stock back to former lower levels.

After assessing the source and nature of the tip, the investor should also assess the stock by itself. Is it worth buying without a "tip"? Is there research available? What is likely to happen if the "tip" doesn't occur? If the stock is more speculative than an investor would normally buy, it should probably be left alone. There are enough good rumors in higher quality stocks to keep one amply busy.

- How does the tip fit into the investment strategy?
- How much risk currently exists with other investments?
- What proportion of the portfolio is in the risk strategy of the overall plan?

Finally, in considering a stock tip, consider how the tip fits into the investment strategy: How much risk currently exists with other investments? What proportion of the portfolio is designated for risk strategy? If certain parameters and dollars have been established in the investor's strategy as "special speculative investment funds," then, by all means, make use of them for any reason. But set a limit as to the amount of risk that will be taken. It is not good to risk everything; it is not good to increase the risk beyond reasonable limits.

Investing in the stock market always has an element of risk. Some risk is rather low and usually has time as an advantage. Other risk is high and strictly short term. Greater risk does not necessarily mean greater potential gain. Some of the greatest gains have come from the fluctuation of interest rates and their effect on the prices of long-term U.S. Treasury bonds. Before investing in high-risk, speculative situations, it can be well worthwhile to ask a few extra questions and take a little time to research the story. This will not eliminate the risk, but it can allow one to enter an investment being aware of the potential risk—an awareness that may prompt one to go in another direction entirely.

Chapter 24

Get Information Before You Invest, Not After

Many of the complicated aspects of our lives could be clarified by asking "why" and finding appropriate information before taking action. Asking why is looked upon as an inconvenience because it calls for analysis, thought and the formulation of a conclusion. These activities can take time and energy. They can lead to unwanted confusion and frustration. To avoid this frustration, many will either depend on the wisdom of others or adopt a "shoot from the hip" approach to dealing with situations.

Depending totally on the "wisdom" of others or "shooting from the hip" can lead to misunderstandings, cause bad timing and be entirely wrong. Investment advice can be helpful, but it can be even more useful as a point of reference rather than being accepted as a total approach. Shooting from the hip is total speculation and gambling.

In the stock market the odds of doing well are increased for the investor who becomes familiar with the current action of the market and the particular stock of interest. Becoming familiar can be accomplished by asking why: Why is the market making this move? Why is this stock an attractive purchase now?

Market Moves

The stock market is a continuous auction with the same product being bought and sold every business day. If there are more buyers, the market and the prices of individual stocks rise in price. If there are more sellers, the market and stock prices drop lower. It's that simple. What makes this simple concept complicated are the factors that motivate the buyers and sellers of stock. Some of these factors are real, others are imagined and still others are fabricated.

A real factor is money. More specifically, the availability of money. Money availability, as it changes with a movement of the interest rates or the earnings of corporations, is one of the most important factors of the stock market.

An imagined factor can be the opinion of a respected economist or market analyst as to current market strength or weakness.

A fabricated factor can be the merciless hammering of computerized sell programs, implemented with the intent of testing market strength by pushing it down as far as possible.

On Friday, October 13, 1989 these market factors came into play simultaneously when a buyout of UAL Corp. failed to obtain the necessary loan approvals (money availability). Some market analysts said this was a sign of further tightening of available money (imagined) and the computer sell programs were activated (fabricated).

The effect was to drop the Dow Jones Industrial Average (DJIA) by 190 points. Fortunately, the Federal Reserve announced that it stood ready with an influx of cash, if needed by the stock market. Confidence returned and the market's retreat was halted. By the end of the year, the market had regained most of the loss and the events of October 13th were being referred to as a sharp correction.

Was this "correction" predictable? Not totally. However there were signs of weakness developing in the market, as shown by the market trends and other indicators.

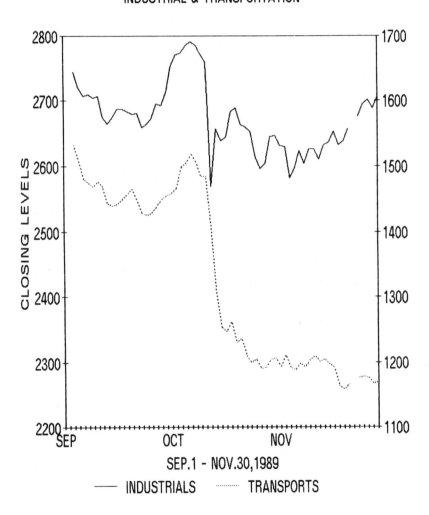

DOW AVERAGES
INDUSTRIAL & TRANSPORTATION

SEP.1 - NOV.30,1989

—— INDUSTRIALS ········ TRANSPORTS

During this time the Dow Transportation Average ran up extraordinarily due to several takeover rumors. This can be observed on the Dow Average movement chart on the preceding page. UAL Corp. was only one of these rumors. It becomes apparent that the DJIA, which had also increased largely due to upward momentum, was much stronger than normal. The increase in the DJIA did not have the added driving force of takeover rumors, so it was quite vulnerable to a market sell-off and a drop.

As is shown by the movement chart, both the Industrials and the Transports peaked on Tuesday, October 10 and began to fall lower. They continued to fall lower during the remainder of the week.

The announcement stating that financing for the UAL Corp. acquisition was being rejected came as an important economic signal. Many analysts said this was a signal of resistance to funding expensive acquisitions. They also said this resistance could lead to higher interest rates in the near future.

Until this signal, money was easily attainable in almost any quantity. The earlier leveraged buyout of another airline, NWA Corp., went through without a hitch. This resistance to borrowing easy money sent a shiver through Wall Street. Resistance could mean higher interest rates, tighter money, and a negative impact on the earnings of all stocks. Lower earnings usually means lower stock prices. This was the incentive for many institutional and individual investors to take some profits and lessen the risk exposure.

The investor who noticed the turn in the stock market by observing the early decline in the Dow Industrials and Transports and listening to the market criticism given by many analysts before Oct. 13 would likely have taken some protective action earlier in the week.

The answer to why the market was advancing had been optimism fueled by leveraged buyouts. Once this optimism started to fade, the averages began to rapidly lose ground. When the UAL Corp. buyout fell through, pessimism took over and the market dropped accordingly. The market correction was more severe than expected, due to the strong selling effects of programmed trading. The market could have corrected just as low without programmed selling, but it probably would not all have happened in one day.

The Dow Industrials and Transports are just two of many market indicators that can help the investor understand strength and direction of market moves.

Stock Moves

Downward Movement. Buying a car or new television set, only to see it on sale the following week, can be a real source of irritation. The same is true of stocks. To pay 40 dollars a share for a stock one day and see the price at 30 a week later is not pleasant. If the investor has valid reasons for the selection to begin with, the stock will generally recover and move on to higher ground. This is often the case, but sometimes the bad news gets worse. An interesting event can occur with a stock which keeps falling.

When a stock price begins to fall, investors will suddenly buy up shares of the stock, at the perceived bargain prices, as others begin selling off their positions of the "declining stock." This is usually shown by the volume surges as the stock drops. Seldom will any of these investors bother to find out why the stock is declining.

The reason for the decline can be serious; lower earnings or estimates, lowered credit rating, or a possible lawsuit or tax problem has developed. The reason for the price decline might not be so serious: market correction, profit taking, employee stock distribution or no news-related reason at all. Whatever the reason for a stock movement, it can be helpful to uncover the information behind the move.

This information about the stock in question can be obtained from the news media or it can be obtained by contacting the company directly. Calling the company might be difficult if hundreds of other investors are trying to do the same thing. Often times a call to the stock broker or a check of the news service on a personal computer will provide the answer as to the reason for the stock's price decline.

Finding out why a stock is declining in price can help the investor decide on the best strategy. That strategy might be a decision to buy, hold or sell, but the information behind the stock move can provide a sound basis for the decision.

Lack of Movement: Why isn't the stock moving? If other similar stocks and the market are doing well, there is a reason for a lack of movement in a given stock. Has there been bad news recently which has created a lack of investor interest or is the stock currently a gem waiting to be discovered? Undiscovered gems can suddenly surge in value when they receive some publicity. Answering these few questions can help the investor decide on the next move.

Why a stock is moving up has some importance.

Upward Movement: Why a stock is moving up is generally important to investors only if they currently don't own it, but might like to be partaking of the profits. Then "why" becomes extra important. Stocks that are increasing in price sometimes make individual investors nervous. No one likes to be holding the bag at the top when the profit taking begins, so they often hesitate, waiting to see if the price will drop to former levels.

If these investors investigate the reason behind the price move, they are better able to make a decision and not waste time nervously waiting. Owners of a stock that is rising do best to pick a reasonable selling point or take protective actions when possible.

Take the time to ask why. Make an inquiry into a stock move or market move. This information should be gathered before the investment decision is made and the action has been implemented. Then the information can be used for making better decisions and setting effective strategy. Asking why increases the odds of making sound and often more profitable investment decisions.

Chapter 25

Never Fight the Tape

Technical analyst Marty Zwieg is an author,[1] newsletter publisher and creator of one of the early "basket funds" (Zwieg Fund; ZF on the New York Stock Exchange).

There are three statements credited to Mr. Zwieg concerning the stock market—statements that contain a great deal of strategic wisdom. The concepts behind the statements have been with investors for many years, but Zwieg has brought the ideas into more current focus:

- "never fight the tape"
- "the trend is your friend"
- "never fight the fed"

"Fight the tape," a term which goes back to earlier days when the progress of the market and individual stocks was tracked by means of the Edison Ticker, which used the famous ticker tape. A series of symbols was communicated to the tickers, which then perforated the paper tape in the shape of these symbols. Business executives and interested investors

---

1   *Winning on Wall Street*, by Marty Zwieg, Warner Books, Inc. 1986. *The Zwieg Forecast*, a newsletter published since 1971.

would have these stock tickers in their offices, where they could keep a close eye on the movement of the stock market.

The reference to "the tape" in the 1990s does not refer to that informative strip of paper, but rather to the trend of the stock market or the price trend of an individual stock. "Fighting the tape," refers to investing contrary to the current trend.

A price trend, once established, represents the current buying or selling sentiment of investors. If the sentiment is favorable and the stock is rising in price, it will continue to rise until the sentiment and actions change. Even though a stock can rise above someone's perception of its current value, buyer sentiment can push the price even higher. No law or principle exists that says the stock must trade within a certain price range. This buying sentiment is usually caused by buyers who are purchasing the stock in the anticipation of improved earnings.

As a stock runs unusually high in price, some skeptics will say the stock is "overbought" and sell short the stock at a new high point. Although this can at times be an accurate assessment—some stocks do retreat from a recent high price—the action can also be similar to stepping in front of a moving train. The train might stop; the stock could retreat. However, if the anticipated earnings growth becomes a reality, the price of the stock could easily continue to rise.

There is a lot of gambling in fighting the trend. It is often true that stocks that have already doubled in value in a bull market are often the first to double in value again. Fighting a trend such as this could be costly. A more effective strategy is to observe the trend and invest in its direction, rather than trying to fight it.

This is not to deny the highly specialized strategy of the "contrarian," who appears to invest against the trend in anticipation of a turn. The actions of the contrarian take experience, discipline and a considerable amount of complicated analysis to be profitable. Even contrarians look for signals of a change in the trend before taking action.

The Trend Is Your Friend

The conclusions drawn from the preceding segment on "never fight the trend" beg similar conclusions with the idea that "the trend is your friend."

The price trend of a stock has a momentum, which will continue as long as investors keep buying the stock. Investors will continue to buy a stock as long as they believe the economy, the stock market and the earnings of that stock will continue to grow at the present rate or better. Although the price of any stock will occasionally run ahead of earnings, the market and the economy (overbought), this does not necessarily mean that the stock should be sold or even sold short. In fact, with a strong stock situation, any price drop may well be a buying opportunity (see Chapter 27).

Mr. Zwieg engages in complicated technical analysis to determine the momentum and strength of a trend. While his analysis enjoys the respect of the financial community, few investors have the time or patience to follow a complicated analysis system. However, investors can benefit by just understanding the basics of not "fighting the tape" or of the trend being a friend.

In considering these two axioms, keep in mind that trends can change. The key is to look for and recognize weakness in a trend as a signal of an approaching turn. This weakness might be observed in the earnings growth of a stock, a weakening trend in the stock market or a developing weakness in the economy. This information is readily available in the financial newspapers or other news media. The investor should follow these developments on a daily basis in order to understand their impact on stock prices.

Never Fight The Fed: Interest rates go up, stock prices go down. Interest rates go down, stock prices go up. These are simple facts. Most stock prices tend to go the opposite direction of interest rates. Most corporations have to borrow some money; when they borrow money, they have to pay interest.

The interest they must pay comes from the earnings they hope to increase by borrowing the money. If they have to pay out more dollars in interest on loans, they obviously have less money in the form of earnings. Consequently, earnings have a direct relationship to the price of the stock: Higher earnings, the stock price goes up. Lower earnings, the stock price goes down.

The only other actions which affect the price of a stock are speculation, which can drive the price higher, or lack of investor interest, which can drive the price lower.

Interest rates are influenced by many changing economic factors and philosophies. The primary source of influence is the action of the Federal Reserve Board (the Fed), which can influence the interest rates charged between banks borrowing from each other in order to meet their reserve requirements. This rate is called the "Federal Funds Rate," or, more simply, "Fed Funds."

Notice that the Fed Funds tend to move with a certain fluidity (see page 122). This daily change of interest rates is influenced by the buying and selling in the bond market, to some extent the action of the stock market and also the apparent attitude of the Federal Reserve Board on the availability of money. Compare this daily movement to the more rigid moves of the Federal Discount Rate on the next page.

The Fed directly controls two other important factors: the federal reserve requirements and the federal discount rate.

The reserve requirements are the dollar amounts required to be maintained in the individual banks. These do not change very often.

The Fed Discount Rate is the rate charged by the Fed to banks that borrow money from them. It is a direct link in the chain of interest rates and the main factor in determining the Prime Rate, which is the interest banks charge their largest borrowers. The Federal Discount Rate can be changed at any time and for any reason. It generally is changed an average of two times a year, however the Fed has no limit as to the number of changes which can be made.[2]

There was a 14 percent rate back in 1981. At this point the Fed had been putting on the brakes trying to slow an economy that had entered an inflationary spiral. The intent was to make money scarce by making it expensive to borrow.

As the economy and inflation slowed, the time came to lower interest rates and step on the gas. By the end of 1982, interest rates had fallen to 8-1/2 percent, by comparison a more reasonable level. The "bubble" in 1984 made many people think that interest rates would again soar. But the Reagan administration had vowed to bring rates lower and force inflation under firm control.

Rates continued to fall. The Federal Discount Rate fell below 6 percent in mid-1986 and stayed there until September 4, 1987. This move up was the first such move in four years and came shortly before the largest stock market drop on October 19, 1987, when the stock market fell more than 500 points in a single day.

There were many reasons for the sharp drop in October of 1987. Many people blamed the raised Discount Rate. Others blamed a weak bond market and panic mutual fund selling. The fact is inflation was creeping back into the economic scene and the Fed was not going to be shy about hitting the brakes to keep the economy from overheating.

Observing *what* is happening with the economy and the stock market can be as important as understanding why things are happening. Observing the current policy and action of the Federal Reserve Board (The Fed) can help the investor go with the current trends rather than fighting against them.

---

2   In 1982, the rate was lowered four times in less than three months, and another three times before the end of the year, for a total of seven lowered rates in less than one year. This was unusual. In 1983, the rate was constant.

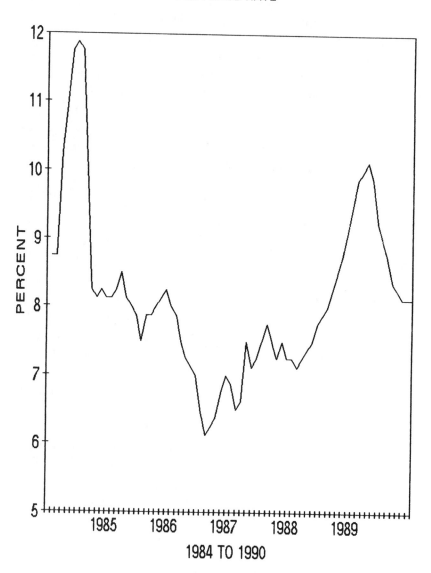

FED FUNDS RATE

FEDERAL DISCOUNT RATE
Federal Reserve Bank of New York

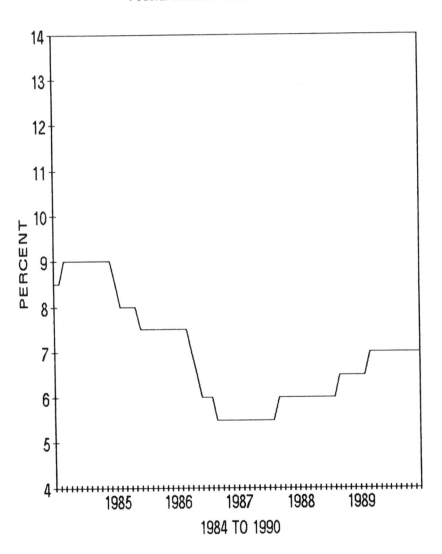

Chapter 26

Heavy Volume, the Price Rises; Light Volume, the Price Falls

The title of this chapter expresses one of those beliefs that on the surface seems to make sense, but does not always stand up to close analysis. It seems logical that a stock will rise in price as investor interest increases and will drop in price as investor interest decreases. This may be true in some situations, but is not always the case.

Take a look at the following stock charts and notice the occasional relationship between volume and increase or decrease in the price of the particular stock.

Notice that the price of IBM did increase as the volume increased (volume shown by the bar chart at the bottom of the graph) in October of 1988. In December, the volume dropped and correspondingly the price dropped in the first two weeks of January. Again toward the end of January the volume showed an increase and the price rose upward. However, with an increase of volume in March, the price showed a significant drop. According to the old wisdom, the volume should have also dropped. In fact, the volume held rather steady since the run up in January, meanwhile the price was falling.

Now look at Kemper Corporation, a company of insurance and mutual funds.

Price Movement Chart: IBM

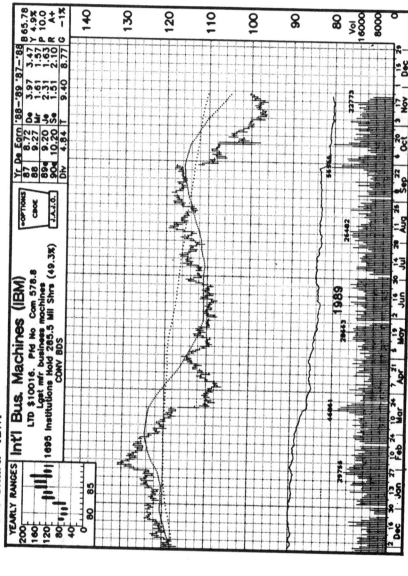

(Chart courtesy of Trendline, a division of Standard & Poor's Corporation. *Daily Action Stock Charts*, November 22, 1989, page 98.)

Price Movement Chart: Kemper Corp.

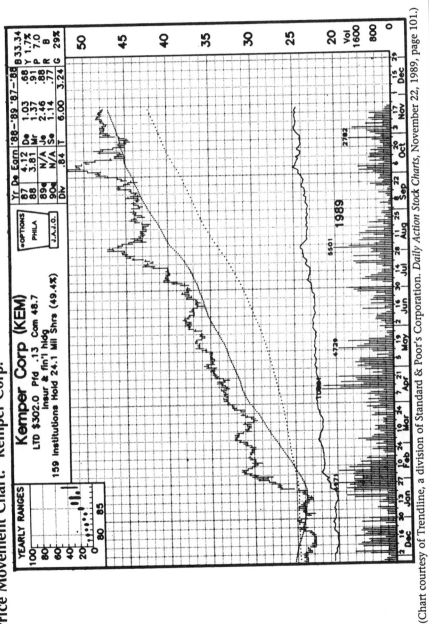

(Chart courtesy of Trendline, a division of Standard & Poor's Corporation. *Daily Action Stock Charts*, November 22, 1989, page 101.)

From October 1988 through the first half of January 1989, the price declined while the volume showed an occasional surge. Volume and price then surged in the end of January and into February. Volume tended to drop off with a good rally every now and then, while the price continued to climb.

The point is, although the volume of trading of individual stocks can at times be significant, it also can be misleading. There are stocks, such as Varity Corp, which can suddenly trade a million or even two million shares in a day and move a modest 1/8 of a dollar in either direction.

Volume as an indicator for individual stocks can be misleading. However, volume as an indicator for the strength of an overall market move can be significant, but there are some surprises. In general, the higher the volume the greater the strength of the market move.

If a market has been averaging 120 million shares a day and staying rather level and suddenly moves up 20 points on 250 million shares, it can be considered a move with considerable strength. If the market moves those same 20 points on volume that is average or below average, the gain is actually showing some weakness. A market move on weak volume can indicate that there are many large investors waiting with skepticism. The likelihood of a reversal is quite high.

Take a look at a New York Stock Exchange volume chart covering a period from Labor Day of 1989 through January of 1990.

It is difficult to see any real trend development as far as gradually increasing or decreasing daily volume. Still, this time period was important and had two major stock market events.

October 13, 1989, the Dow Industrials dropped more than 190 points in a single day. This is easy to find on the volume graph. It is near where the volume jumped to over 400 million shares traded—near the day but not *on* the day. Actually the volume on October 13th was only 251 million shares. The heavy volume was the following Monday, when the market traded 416 million shares.

TOTAL DAILY VOLUME
NEW YORK STOCK EXCHANGE

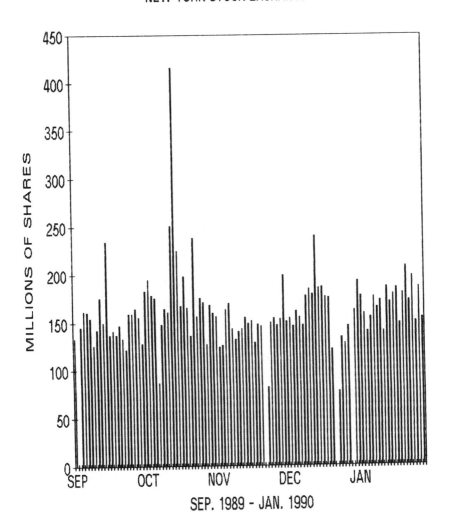

SEP. 1989 - JAN. 1990

The second event during this time period was an all-time new high for the DJIA. This event is not so obvious in just looking at the volume. Most people remember that it was the first business day of 1990 when the Dow set another record, closing at 2810.15. The lack of heavy volume showed a lack of strength in this rally of the Dow Industrials. This lack of strength signalled a likely turn in the market and the market did drop.

Volume itself doesn't seem to indicate much in the way of useful information. Changes in volume and surprises in volume are another story. Now, take a look at the same volume chart in comparison to the DJIA

Notice the volume for January 2. It was quite modest, just a little above the average. The stock market cannot seem to sustain a rally without the support of strong volume. The lack of volume and other weak market indicators brought sellers to the market and the DJIA began a decline that lasted the rest of the month.

Notice the lack of volume back in late September of 1989 when the DJIA was reaching toward a new high. In fact, nearly all of the increased volume spikes appearing on this graph were not during market rallies, but rather periods of declining corrections. Heavier volume on market downward corrections is often a bearish sign.

When the stock market rallies on relatively light volume, it tends to retreat soon after due to a lack of buyer support. This failure to build volume on gains is often a buildup of bearish sentiment.

There are market analysts who measure up volume vs. down volume as an indicator of investor sentiment. This leads to different momentum measurements which are only occasionally accurate. The problem with most of these volume measures is their dependence on number systems which are (based on) generalities rather than on what is actually happening in the market. Another weakness is their tendency to narrowly focus attention on only one, two or three indicators for signals. The close view on only a small number of indicators, which are strongly dependent on numeric systems, usually leaves room for a lot of error and misunderstandings.

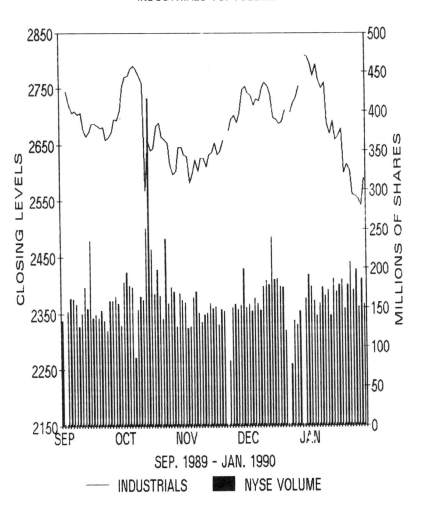

DOW AVERAGES
INDUSTRIALS VS. VOLUME

SEP. 1989 - JAN. 1990

—— INDUSTRIALS   ■ NYSE VOLUME

Volume *can* indicate an increase of investor interest. While this is a fair statement, it is necessary to look for the cause of the interest and the impact on the stock or the market as a whole. Looking at overall volume in a market move, whether up or down, can tell the individual investor a great deal as to the strength of the current sentiment. If the market tends to rise on strong volume and fall on light volume, the sentiment can be considered bullish. If, however, a rally fails to bring strong volume with the move, a turning point might be signaled.

Chapter 27

Buy on Weakness—Sell on Strength

Buying on weakness should only take place after it has been determined that the stock is still a fundamentally sound investment. Many investors have had the unpleasant experience of buying a stock that has declined in price only to see it drop further. So, what is "weakness" and how is it determined?

Once a stock has been selected as a potential investment, if it is a good stock in a relatively good to balanced market, the stock will move up in surges and then hesitate. It will often drift lower, looking for the support of new buyers, then it will advance again. This hesitation and drifting is caused by the exit of early profit takers.

Many times this "weakness" is found in the company that has possibly announced stock buy back programs (and actually does buy back the stock) or could have recently increased the dividend payout. It is the stock which had good earnings for the same period of time of the previous year. The earnings picture on this stock probably looked positive for the past three years and five years. It is the stock of a company that can handle the debt situation and has a strong balance sheet. It is the stock of a company that is well managed and knows its position in the market. A company that sticks to the knitting of what it does well, rather than diversifying for the sake of diversification. It is a company that is or will likely become a dominant force within its own industry.

Take a look at Waste Management (WMX), a stock that trades on the New York Stock Exchange.

Price Movement Chart: Waste Management

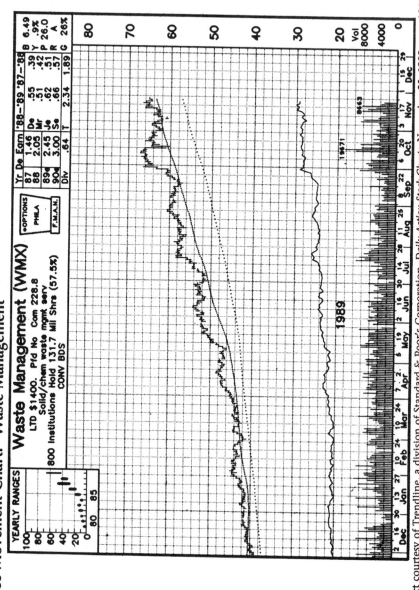

(Chart courtesy of Trendline, a division of Standard & Poor's Corporation. *Daily Action Stock Charts*, November 22, 1989, page 184.)

Note the steady climb of Waste Managements price through 1986 and 1987. The price leveled out after the severe market correction in October of 1987 and began to climb once again. Note the step-like nature of the advancing price. These steps are the areas which could be used for "buying on weakness."

Selling on strength is one of those ideas which sounds good, makes a lot of sense and is very difficult to actually implement. The reason for the difficulty is a perceived conflict with the concept of "letting the winners run."

Actually there is no conflict if the decision to sell the stock has been made for sound value reasons. If the investor believes that the value has declined due to an increase in price without a corresponding increase in earnings or potential earnings, then one merely waits for a small rally and sells.

Selling into strength increases the probability of a favorable trade execution. For example:

QUOTE: APT CORP.

Last	Change	Bid	Ask	Volume
21	+1 1/4	20 7/8	21 1/8	415,345

The stock is up $1.25 on comparatively heavy volume (average daily volume 85,000 shares). With a quarter spread between the bid and ask, a market order to sell 500 shares will likely fill between the two prices or even higher. A limit order could be used, but if the stock is above the price objective of 20 dollars a share, a market order will save valuable time. Selling on strength is usually enough finesse without adding the possible complications of a limit order.

Buying on weakness and selling on strength should be looked at as a matter of finesse rather than a total strategy. This finesse enables the investor to be more in control of the situation. It is the taking of a direct action rather than reacting to a market situation.

At times the market will not allow finesse when it is moving strongly against the investor. Then it is time to take action at the earliest possible moment. But during those times when the investor is in control, finesse can add a few extra dollars to each transaction and make the experience of investing much more enjoyable.

Chapter 28

It Is Best to Trade "At the Market"

Market orders have priority. This simple fact is important to remember. Market orders say that the investor is willing to buy or sell stock at the "best available price."

This order will, by its very nature, take precedence over any other kind of order. It must be presented to the "trading crowd" by the specialist on the New York Stock Exchange (or other exchange) at the earliest possible moment. There can be other market orders ahead of the current order, but it does take precedence over limit orders as well as all other types of orders. Market orders on listed stock (trading on a stock exchange) often go through the Designated Order Turnaround (DOT) system, which immediately matches buys and sells and returns a report of order execution.

Implications of a Market Order

A market order implies the investor's desire for a fast execution; it says that the investor wants to buy or sell as quickly as possible. This is likely to happen as the market order takes precedence over all other types of orders.

A market order also implies any price will be acceptable. This is often forgotten until an investor pays more than expected for a stock purchase or receives less than expected on a sell. If an investor is buying 100 shares at market, that investor is effectively saying that he or she will buy that stock at any price. Under steady, evenly paced market conditions, this buy will be made at or near the current quoted offer on the stock (at or near the bid showing on a sell).

In a "fast market" situation the investor could pay a few dollars or several dollars more per share when buying. This can be of extra concern in a buy-out situation, where 20 or 60 or more dollars extra per share might be paid with a market order.

A market order also implies a willingness to pay more than one price for a block of stock. Round lots of 100 shares are generally filled at the same price. A multiple round lot of 200, 500 or 10,000 shares could be filled at different prices, for each of the hundred share round lots. This is most often a problem with stocks which are "thinly traded," meaning they trade in low daily volumes or might not trade every day.

For example, an investor wishes to purchase 1000 shares of Damp Corp. at the market. The current price quote looks something like this:

BUY: 1000 Damp Corp. at the market.

Quote:

Symbol	Last Trade	Bid	Ask	Volume
DMP	41	40 7/8	41	1400

As the order is filled it is possible for the following to occur:

	Quantity	Purchase Price	Cost
	500 shares	41	$20,500
	200 shares	41 1/8	8,225
	300 shares	41 1/4	12,375
Total:	1000 shares		$41,100

The above investor paid 100 dollars more than expected on a purchase of 1,000 shares. This is a legitimate filling of the market order. Some investors claim to protect themselves by checking "the size" of the order. The size tells the number of round lots available on the current bid and on the current offer. However, size can often be misleading as the size can change in an instant as preceding orders alter its status. Also, the size might not be of sufficient quantities to accommodate a particular order.

There are implications with a market order which the investor should be aware of when trading stocks. The possibility of paying any price or the chance of paying more than one price are disadvantages. These order executions can happen with any stock but tend to occur most often with stocks that trade with low daily volumes. However, in most cases, the advantage of an immediate execution outweighs the disadvantages of a market order.

Chapter 29

The Type of Order Can Be As Important As the Order

There are many different types of stock orders that can be placed. Some of the different types are of debatable value and are seldom used. Below are descriptions of some of the basic types of orders stated in a simplified form.

Orders for Buys or Sells

Market Order: Best available price.

Limit Order: Specific acceptable price.

Stop Order:[1] Best available price once the stop price is traded on or through.

Stop Limit Order: Specific acceptable price once the stop price is traded on or through. The limit price can be placed at the same price or at an entirely different price from the stop price.

---

1   The most used and most important types of orders, for the individual investor, are the market, limit and stop orders.

Market If Touched: Becomes a market order if the set price is traded on or through. Buy orders are placed below current market price, sell orders are placed above current market price. (This placement is the opposite of stop orders.)

Market On Open: Specifies the market open as an activator. Obviously, this order must be placed before the market has begun trading. It is a market order and does not necessarily guarantee the opening price.

Market On Close: Specifies near the closing price (note that it is also called a "market" order.) The order must be placed before the market closes trading. Filled in the last few minutes of trading.

Chapter 30

Order Modifications Might Cause Delay

Careful consideration should be given to any modification placed on an order. An order with any qualifiers other than market order, can take extra time to be executed.

Good Till Cancelled: The order stays in place until it is filled, cancelled, changed by the investor or cancelled by the broker. Brokerage firms have different rules as to the total time period they will carry a "good till cancelled" (GTC) order on their books. Also referred to as an "open order," it will usually be carried 30 days or will be good until the end of the next month. At the end of the time period the order is automatically cancelled. This helps people remember the pending order and prevents duplication of orders. The policy also gets rid of orders that do not have a reasonable chance of being filled in the near future.

At any time, the person placing the order may cancel or change the order, although some firms have rules as to the number of times an order can be changed. It is costly and somewhat risky to continually change modified orders. Instructions can be confused and misunderstood, leading to unhappy customers and frustrated brokerage firms.

Buy orders and stop orders generally have the modifier "DNR" added to GTC orders. DNR means simply do not reduce. Most investors want an order filled even if it has gone

EX dividend and reduced the price. Firms will often require the DNR modification on all applicable GTC orders. If the GTC order has not been executed or cancelled by the end of the time period (set by the firm), it is automatically cancelled.

If the investor wishes to change an open order, it is important to notify the broker of the current order. If two orders are placed, two orders will be filled. One does not automatically cancel the other.

The advantage to the "Good Till Cancelled" order is its automatic nature. The order stays in effect day after day and does not have to be reentered. The disadvantage to an open order is the possibility of delay. The order will be filled when it is possible to obtain an execution. There might be several nearly identical orders ahead which have to be filled first. These orders, known as "stock ahead," can cause frustrating delays for the investor.

Market orders are automatically "day order," but may be entered "good till cancelled" on very thinly traded stocks. Some preferred stocks and small company stocks might not trade every day.

Day Order: The "Day Order" is just what it says. It is an order good for the day only. If the order cannot be executed by the end of the trading day, it is cancelled. A notice of the cancellation is sent to the broker "firm nothing done," who in turn notifies the investor. The order can be changed or cancelled at any time during the trading day.

The frequent trader of stocks is likely to use day orders just to decrease record keeping. Also the desirability of a stock play could be significantly altered as quickly as the next day, when the investor might have a different strategy altogether. The main disadvantage of the day order can be waiting for a firm "nothing done" to be reported.

Or Better: The term "or better" refers to the advantage of the investor. It is a limit order to buy that is placed at or above the current offer; or a limit order to sell that is placed at or below the current bid price. For example, the stock ABX is trading currently at 21 1/4 and is up 1 1/4 from the closing price of 20 dollars a share from the previous day. The full quote looks like this:

Symbol	Last	Change	Bid	Ask
ABX	21 1/4	+ 1 1/4	21	21 1/4

The investor wishes to buy ABX and take advantage of a possible continuing uptrend in price. However, the investor realizes that a market order can fill above the current offer showing. The investor is willing to pay as much as 21 1/2 dollars for the stock but doesn't want to pay the high price unless it is absolutely necessary. The order is entered as a limit, or better. The order is entered:

Buy 500 shares ABX at a limit of 21 1/2 or better, *day order.*

If the order can be executed within the modifiers, the investor will pay 21 1/2 dollars or less per share. If the price moves and stays above the 21 1/2 dollars per share before this investor's order can be filled, this limit or better order will not be filled and will be cancelled at the end of the day.

Orders with the modifier "or better" can be placed directly on the current offer showing or at any higher level. They would be inappropriate below the current offer showing on the quote. "Or better" is automatically assumed for any limit buy order placed below the current offer showing.

The advantage of the "or better" order is the control of the price. The disadvantage is the possible lack of execution.

All or None: "All or none" can be used with multiple round lot or block orders. Generally a guideline of 1000 shares or more is sufficient to make use of the modifier "all or none." Its purpose is to prevent partial fills of an order.

For example, a person wishes to buy 1000 shares of BBB Corporation at 20 dollars a share. The stock is currently trading 19 7/8 bid to 21 1/8 ask. If the order is entered as a limit of 20 dollars, it might only be possible to fill 500 or maybe 600 shares during the day. If the modifier of "all or none" is added, there are only two possibilities at the end of the trading day: the investor bought 1000 shares of BBB at 20 dollars a share or the order was not executed.

Even though a partial fill might be desirable in some situations, in most cases the investor would rather have the total quantity. If limit orders are entered "good till cancelled," a separate, full commission could be charged for each day a partial fill occurs, thereby increasing costs.

The main advantage to the "all or none" modifier is control of the filled quantity. It must be filled at the same time and price. The main disadvantage is the possible lack of execution even though the stock might trade at the limit price.

Immediate or Cancel: Also known as "fill or kill," this order modifier is added to a limit that is at or close to an executable price. If the order cannot be filled immediately it is cancelled and the report is sent to the broker. It is a modifier that tends to be used with larger trades tempting the specialist or trading desk to implement the filling of the order.

Not Held: This is a market order modifier that allows the floor broker a time advantage to obtain a more favorable price if possible. The advantage is possibly a better price execution. The disadvantage is the market might move against the order and give an execution that is unfavorable. The investor accepts the risk on this order.

Note: There can be times of fast markets where some firms will only accept "market not held" orders. This occurred during the severe market correction in October of 1987. Due to a "late tape" (the clearing of orders was behind its normal pace) price quotations were late and unreliable, and there was no way to know at what price an order might be filled.

Odd Lot On Sale: Occasions can arise where an investor has a combination of a round lot (hundred share amount) and an odd lot (less than 100 shares) of stock. An amount such as 425 shares of XYZ Company would be a combination round lot/odd lot. This can be the case with employee stock purchase plans or it could be the result of a stock split.

If a limit order is placed on the sell of the stock, the investor might wish to consider adding the modifier "odd lot on sale." This effectively says the round lot must be executed at the limit price and then the odd lot can be sold "at market." This strategy greatly simplifies the transaction. The odd lot (less than 100 shares) could be charged a customary additional fee of 1/8 dollar (12 1/2 cents) per share. This is called the "odd lot differential."

If a limit sell order is placed, the price will have to be at a level that also covers the odd lot differential fee, thus complicating and possibly delaying the order execution. This is true unless the "Odd Lot On Sale" is added as a modifier.

Placing a combination round lot/odd lot limit with odd lot on sale has the advantage of an easier and faster execution. The only possible disadvantage is accepting a lower price on the odd lot portion of the order.

Modifiers such as price limits, "all or none," or "immediate or cancel" can have an effect on the ease of execution of an order. There can be sound reasons for placing limit orders or other modifiers on orders, but in most cases the time saved by placing market orders more than makes up for the time lost waiting for another eighth of a dollar. Placing market orders can save an investor time and money.

Chapter 31

Remember, Others Might Have the Same Idea

Sometimes a great deal of analysis goes into the decision of trading a particular issue of stock. No matter what the conclusion—buy, hold, set a limit or stop order—the chances are several other investors have the same idea. More importantly, these "competitors" might have placed their orders previously.

One example of this "same idea" phenomena is illustrated by the fact that most limit orders are placed on whole numbers, halves and quarters. They are placed on eighths less often. This competition can create a problem: If there are other orders ahead, the current limit order might not be filled. Other orders "at the market" can move the stock price in such a way that only some of the limit orders ahead are executed. The market price then moves away from the investors limit, still driven by market orders.

Another example of the "same idea" problem can be seen when a buy-out offer appears overnight. The stock might have closed at 56 and the buy-out offer is 75 dollars a share. Many investors want to buy the stock on the open at the closing 56 dollar a share level. This is usually not possible. The stock will generally build up a large supply of "market" orders to buy and will open near or even above the buy-out price.

When implementing a strategy it is important to keep in mind that other investors might have the same idea. Rather than following a more popular strategy, an investor is better off selecting a slightly different tactic. Placing a limit order on eighths might have a better chance of being filled: a limit order to sell 100 shares at 21 3/8 rather than 21 1/2, is less likely to have others competing for the same price. If the order is not filled in a reasonable time it can be changed to a market order. This sort of contingency planning can help the investor avoid unwanted delays.

Chapter 32
Use Limit Orders
As Insurance

Limit orders can be used as insurance against a buy order being executed at a price higher than expected and they can be used as a strategy of "bottom fishing" with a stock that has been declining in price. The main risk is that the order will not be filled and the stock will not be purchased. If the buy order is not filled it can be a lost opportunity, but is not a loss of real money. There are always other stocks to buy.

Limits on the sell side can be a different story, real losses can occur if the order is not executed. Limit sell orders should be placed with a great deal of caution. This is especially true with a stock that has been declining in price. Profits are declining, dollars are evaporating. The investor still owns the stock and begins lowering the limit, still trying to hang on to a few extra dollars. This is risky and often filled with frustration.

Limit orders are best used as a kind of insurance against an unexpected market move or on a stock in a fast market. When the stock quotation appears on the computer screen it is already history. There are no rules for market orders to be filled at the current quote. A little protection could be in order for the unusually volatile stock.

For example: ABC stock is showing a bid price of 25 dollars a share. The offer (buy price) is 25 1/8. Some investors will be tempted to place an order to buy one hundred shares at 25. This strategy, which might take some time to execute, will save the investor 12 1/2 cents per share and the order might never fill.

If the investor wants to buy the stock and stay in control of the situation, the order should be placed on the offer of 25 1/8. Placing the buy order, with a limit price on the offer would look like the example below, which illustrates buying in a slow to moderate market:

Price Quote:

Stock	Last	Change	Bid	Ask	Volume
ABC	25	+1/8	25	25 1/8	30,000

Buy: 100 shares ABC
25 1/8 limit
Day

This order has a high likelihood of being executed. The stock is up a small amount on moderate volume. If the order were placed as a market order, the fill could be identical to the limit. However, look at the following situation, which illustrates buying in a fast market, where the limit is truly protective: For example: Buying in a fast market:

Stock	Last	Change	Bid	Ask	Volume
ABC	25	+ 2 1/8	25	25 1/4	130,000

Buy: 500 shares ABC
25 1/4 limit
Day

This order has a chance of being filled, but as fast as the price is moving, backed by heavy volume, it could be difficult to fill. The limit will prevent the order from causing an up tick to 25 3/8 or 25 1/2, although it might not be possible to fill the order.

The investor can increase the chances of an execution by setting the price higher than the current offer and adding the modifier "or better" (such as "25 1/2 or better"). This would greatly increase the probability of an order execution and insure a price of no more than 25 1/2 dollars a share.

Below is an example of selling in a slow to moderate declining market:

Price Quote:

Stock	Last	Change	Bid	Ask	Volume
ABC	25	-1/8	25	25 1/8	30,000

Sell: 100 shares ABC
25 limit
Day

Placing the limit on the current bid showing helps to insure an execution and does prevent the stock from selling on a down tick. If it is time to sell the stock, it should be sold on the bid, or at market. This is not the time to try and squeeze another 12 1/2 cents a share out of this security.

Compare this to selling stock in a declining, fast market:

Stock	Last	Change	Bid	Ask	Volume
ABC	25	-2 1/8	25	25 1/4	130,000

Sell: 500 shares ABC
25 limit
Day

A market sell order of 500 shares could cause a down tick and execution of 24 3/4 or even 24 1/2 (depending on orders ahead). Normally it would down tick 1/8 per trade, but only three orders ahead of this sell could push it that low. Also, a fast market such as this can down tick the price at a larger rate. The limit price of 25 will insure the price, but will not insure an execution of the order. If the order is not quickly executed and the price continues to drop, the investor might wish to change this sell to a market order.

Implications of a Limit Order

- A limit order implies that the investor is willing to wait as long as necessary for the order to be filled. It might take an hour, a day, a week or the order might never be filled.

- A limit order of multiple round lots implies that the investor will accept part of the order being filled. The investor can avoid this partial filling by placing the modifier "all or none" on the order, although this could make the order even more difficult to fill.

- A limit order often implies that the investor believes the stock will move opposite to its current direction and will then resume. This is the way many limit orders are placed even though the strategy and the action are not in a line. The stock has risen 1 1/2 dollars, but the buyer wants to save an eighth or a quarter and places such a limit below the current offer. This can cause problems as a strategy because often times, when the order is filled and the stock is purchased, the excitement is over and the stock drops.

- A limit order implies that the investor will accept the order being filled at that price or a better price. The term "or better" need only be applied when the investor is placing a limit price above the current offer on a buy or below the current bid on a sell.

Chapter 33
Values Can Be Found Bottom Fishing

Bottom fishing is a technique of using a limit buy order to purchase a stock that has been going through difficult times and has shown a significant price decline.

The stock itself might currently be out of favor or the industry could be having its own recession. Cyclical stocks such as car companies, oils, heavy equipment and to some extent food, all lend themselves to bottom fishing. Industries such as airlines, computers and defense equipment manufacturers tend to go out of favor from time to time. When this happens, the bottom fishers come out in force. They grab their long-term price charts to see how low the price went during the last down cycle. They assess the current market situation, pick a price target and place their limit orders. The objective is to pay a price as close to the bottom as possible.

It once was said on Wall Street that a market bottom was near (after a decline) when one could see well-dressed aged men or women, walking quickly (though often with some difficulty) to the brokerage offices to buy their favorite stocks at bargain prices. These were the experienced bottom fishers and it was believed that a market rally would soon be seen. This indicator disappeared with the advent of the telephone.

Bottom fishing can be highly speculative because there is no way of knowing how low the price of a stock will eventually fall. The strategy is most effective in an overall market decline. It can be riskier in an individual stock situation. If a stock was at 80 about a year ago and is now at 45 will it go to 40 or will it keep dropping to 25? Even if the investor sees a low price of 39 during the last down cycle, there is no assurance this will be repeated. This is the risk a bottom fisher is willing to take. If the investor is correct in the strategy it can bring great profits.

Chapter 34

Heavily Margined—Heavily Watched

Margin is borrowing money, using stocks or other securities (which have been fully paid for) as collateral. These borrowed funds can be used for any purpose (the cash can be withdrawn by the investor), although the money is most commonly used to buy more stock or other securities.

Margin can be a useful tool to leverage investments for greater profits. Simply put, it works something like this: the investor puts up one half the value of the stock purchased (current Regulation-T requires 50 percent of the value at the time of the transaction). For example, to buy 200 shares of POW Corporation at 106 dollars per share:

Total Cost:	$21,200
Investor puts in	10,600
Amount borrowed	$10,600 (margin debit)

If the price of POW Corp. goes to 150 dollars per share, it will be worth 30,000 dollars. The investor owes only the margin debit and whatever interest has accumulated (the debit is a loan, interest is only charged for the days the debt is outstanding). In this POW Corp. example, the investor still owes the debit of 10,600 dollars:

Current value, 150 dollars per share

Total value	$30,000
Debit owed	10,600
Investor's equity	$19,400

If the investor sells the position and takes profits, the picture could look like this:

Investor's value	$19,400*
Original investment	10,600
Profit	$ 8,800 **

(* After the margin debit is repaid.)
(** No adjustment made for any interest owed. No adjustment made for commissions)

Essentially the investor has doubled the gain through leverage by buying twice as many shares with half of them purchased by means of a loan. Although the maximum of 50 percent loan value is used in this example it is allowable to borrow less than this amount.

This is fine as long as the price of the stock goes up in value. The problems with margin occur as the price begins to drop. What if instead of rising in price, POW Corp. fell to 50 dollars a share?

200 POW Corporation	
50 dollars per share	$10,000
Margin debit owed	10,600***
Investor's value	-$ 600

(*** The amount of the debit remains constant. Debit is unaffected by market price changes.)

If the investor sold out at 50 dollars a share, not only would the original investment of 10,600 be totally lost, but the investor would owe an additional 600 dollars. This is reason enough to carefully watch margined positions.

In actuality the investor would receive margin maintenance calls before this low level is reached, although in a rapidly declining market there might not be enough time to bring in the additional funds necessary to cover the margin call. Maintenance calls can request immediate delivery of funds. In less volatile markets, sufficient time is granted; but in fast moving markets, maintenance calls can be due the same day.

Required margin maintenance on stocks is currently 25 percent equity, however brokerage firms will generally require 30 and even 40 percent equity. Brokerage firms are allowed to set more strict requirements for margin maintenance. This means that the investor must have cash enough to maintain ownership of at least 30 to 40 percent of the value of the stocks on margin. Margin calls can be satisfied with a deposit of cash or other fully paid marginable securities, which the investor already owns.

If the required margin is not maintained, the brokerage firm has every right to sell the stocks or other securities in the account to prevent a further loss of value. This was a common problem in the October 1987 market crash. Investors, many of whom were on vacation, suddenly found their stock portfolios, once worth hundreds of thousands of dollars, totally gone. In fact, many of them still owed substantial amounts of money to the brokerage firm.

"Heavily margined——heavily watched" is a market axiom well worth remembering and following. It is also wise to protect the margin position when necessary. Total protection is not possible, but a few precautions can lessen the blow in a severe decline.

Protect the margin position with careful and deliberate attention. Brokers are continually amazed as to the number of people who will make a stock purchase just before leaving on vacation. It is like some special list of things to do: stop the mail, load the car, get the kids and buy some stock. This is usually not a good time to buy any stock, but it can be exactly the wrong time to increase a margin position. A lot can happen to the stock market in a week or two and most people on vacation have enough to do without keeping an eye on the stock market.

Margin can be used with minimal risk and maximum impact, but it requires care and attention. Margin positions can be maintained by using the strategies described below:

Daily Observation: Keep an eye on the market situation every day by computer, calling the broker and watching the papers.

Extra Precautions: Take extra precautions when leaving town on a vacation or business trip. Consider arrangements (with the broker) for someone to bring money or securities to cover any possible maintenance calls. Keep in touch. It can be a good idea to totally pay off the margin debit during this time.

Placing Protective Orders: This could be a good situation for stop loss sell orders.

Selling Margined Positions: Keep only the fully paid for securities and reduce the margin debit to zero. This would eliminate the possibility of any margin calls. This can be extra important when leaving for an extended period of time.

Being Extra Cautious With A Short Position: A short position has a potentially unlimited risk since there is no limit to how high the price of a stock can rise. Carefully placed buy stop orders can help control this risk.

Margin can be a useful tool for leverage when buying stocks and other securities. It should be used carefully and deliberately. The investor should have a basic understanding of the workings of margin before making use of this leverage. It is possible to learn more about margin by asking the broker for information or by looking for one of the many good books on the subject.

Chapter 35

Winners Keep On Winning

Winners often keep on winning. They will usually keep on winning as long as the factors that make them a winner remain in effect. Some winners, however, will run until they drop.

From the individual's viewpoint, the concept of a stock running until it drops might be experienced when the investor hangs on to a stock that should be sold, whether to take profits or prevent losses. In each situation, there is a balance between having the patience to wait for the expected results and taking the action to close out a position. Differences in individuals and lack of similarity in market situations make this balance difficult to determine. It is a technique to be developed through experience and observation. It is a technique of timing, and timing is the key to consistent profits.

It is important for the investor to develop a profit and loss plan as should be done with any business venture. The plan need not be complicated. It should be well defined and yet have some flexibility in order to take advantage of exceptions. Here is a simple profit and loss plan:

Take profits at: 18 to 20 percent
(except in special situations)

Take losses at: 8 to 10 percent

This is a very general plan and will not be complete enough for most investors, but it is a plan for profit and loss. The special situations can be a cause for raising the profit-taking price, but require some solid reasons for the raised objective. The idea is to win big, rather than riding a stock up and riding it back down.

Most investors would like to find what Peter Lynch refers to as a "tenbagger":

- Buying 3-M at a dollar a share
- Buying Microsoft at 19 dollars a share
- Buying Alza at 4 dollars a share . . .

These are the kinds of "winners" investors are looking to buy. Many stockbrokers will tell of individuals who have the assets and the desire to invest in stocks, but are constantly looking for that special stock which will triple or quadruple in a year or so. They often never buy any stock and the money just sits in a money market fund drawing below average interest rates.

These would-be investors become so obsessed with the large gain on a single stock that they end up either buying no stock at all or go to the other extreme and buy a speculative stock which turns to "tapioca."

Stocks which have been "tenbaggers" in the past can still be good stocks. In fact many like 3-M and Microsoft continue to have substantial growth year after year. Winners do often keep on winning and an investor with a longer term objective will do well to buy some strong winners.

"Tenbaggers" are wonderful. The buyers have a conversation topic for the next several years. Every investor would like to tie into one of the "hotter" issues of stock. Although some investors seem to have a knack for picking hot stocks, in many cases, those who bought such a marvelous stock did so by accident. They didn't know at the time that the stock would be so successful.

If an investor has the savvy, experience and informational resources of Peter Lynch, it might be possible to find a few super stocks and do well by trading in them. However, most investors do not have the luxury of devoting all of their time to the study of successful stocks. Most people have to work a regular job and spend at least some time with friends and family. This makes stalking the tenbagger a difficult task.

Tripping over a "tenbagger" is wonderful luck, but achieving a price objective in a carefully selected "winner" stock is also a wonderful experience. The prudent and the astute investors are pleased with a little extra luck, but they are always planning strategy to achieve objectives that are not so dependent on luck.

Chapter 36

Indicators Can Meet Overriding Factors

"No matter what the current indicators are saying, they can be overridden by other, unexpected factors."

S. A. Nelson

On Friday, May 11, 1990, the Dow Industrials rallied more than 63 points. This was an unusual rally that surprised many investors. It was a surprise because most of the stock market indicators were signalling a market which was growing weaker.

The Industrials, Transports and Utilities had been drifting apart. The Transportation Average did not participate in the January 2 rally, which sent the Industrials to a new high of 2810. The Utility Average had been drifting lower since the preceding December. Volume had been dropping lower. Interest rates had been creeping up and the market continued to weaken.

This was the Friday when the Producer Pric ₃ Index came out and showed a .3 decline. The Index is often used as a measure of actual inflation, it had been creeping higher since the latter part of 1989.

The decline of the Producer Price Index was a good-news shot in the arm for the stock market. What had been a slow and drifting market became like a raging bull. The upward move existed not only in the Dow Averages, but also spread to the broader market. Advancing stocks led declining stocks nearly four to one. The volume on the New York Stock Exchange climbed to more than 250 million shares (the average volume had been running about 90 million shares a day).

This was truly an example where the growing negative indicators were overridden by one positive change. Often it is the positive indicators that are overwhelmed by some negative event. Here are some examples of the kind of happening which might have enough significance to override the current positive stock market indicators:

- Funding for a large project can fail at the last minute, sending the entire market into a spin.
- A U.S. Treasury bond auction might not go as well as expected and cause interest rates to rise.
- An earthquake, flood, fire, hurricane or other calamity can unexpectedly send the market down.
- A war can break out.
- A national scandal can suddenly hit the news.
- The dollar may suddenly weaken and fall too low.
- Interest rates might suddenly be raised.

Any of these, and many other surprise events, can appear and cause the stock market to suddenly change direction. This can happen even when all of the indicators are showing a strong or stable market or it can occur when all of the indicators are signalling weakness. This is why news and information are so very important in the stock market.

It has been said that, "Information makes the market." Actually, what makes the market is the reaction (shown by an increase of buying and selling) or lack of reaction to the information. The stock market will often rise on good news and fall on bad news. At times, when bad news is expected, the market often ignores the information; this happens because the market has already discounted the news. Understanding the possible impact of economic news and being aware of that news can give considerable advantages to the individual investor. This is why it is also important to understand the current themes and informational concerns of the current stock market.

Understanding what scares the investors or what currently gets them excited can help the individual investor make investment selections with better timing. Although the market indicators are important, it is also necessary for the individual to be aware of the fact that the indicators can be overridden by other events.

Chapter 37

Take a Loss Quickly

"If it were done when 'tis done, then 'twere well it were done quickly."

Macbeth.[1]

Taking a loss is not a pleasant task. No one likes to do it at all. If one is to be an active investor it will become necessary to take a loss from time to time. Most of Wall Street's big players from past years believed they only had to be correct about *half* of the time. It is inevitable that the necessity of taking a loss will face the individual investor.

If the decision has been made to take the loss, this is not the time to try and get something a little extra to soften the blow. There are novice investors who have decided to take a loss on a stock and at the last minute place a limit sell order just above the current trading range. In most cases, the order is never filled and the stock either just sits there or drops lower. As time passes the number of these limit sell orders, just above the current market price, begin to grow in number.

This gathering of limit sell orders creates a phenomena called *overhead supply*. Even if good news is forthcoming, the stock will have a difficult time rallying through all of those limit sell orders. It is possible that the overhead supply will begin to drift lower. The members of the group (all with the same idea) realize the difficulty of the situation and begin to

---

1   Shakespeare's *Macbeth*, Act I, Scene VII.

lower their limit prices. Some of these sell orders are executed and the price is driven even lower. This predicament can become time consuming and frustrating for the investor.

The solution is simple. Once the decision has been made to sell and take the loss it should be done as quickly as possible. The money will then be available for purchasing better investments. The market sell order will accomplish this with the greatest speed.

Chapter 38

Beware the Triple Witching Hour

The third Friday of every month is the last day to trade stock options. Actual options expiration is on Saturday, but it is often the expiration of trading which can cause concern. Unusual volatility can occur in this third week of the month due to the unwinding of options positions. At times this volatility seems unrelated to any of the usual market indicators, but rather exists by itself.

March, June, September and December are even more important on the third week due to additional options expirations. These expirations are for stock, futures and index options.

The term "triple witching" comes from the high volatility patterns that can develop in the third week of the above listed months. In recent years new regulations and the promise of stricter controls have helped to moderate the situation, but the potential for a hyperactive market during these times still exists. If significant economic news comes out at the same time as these expirations, the volatility can be magnified.

During this time many of the large options traders are selling out of the expiring options and buying other option positions that are not expiring. This keeps the action in the options.

Occasionally stocks become more attractive and the money goes into stocks, driving the market in an upward direction. At other times, the options are more attractive and stock positions will be sold to buy more options. This can drive the market lower. The situation can drive the market into a sharp correction. Some of the sharp corrections in 1985 and 1986 were attributed to "the triple witching hour."

The individual investor should be aware of options expiration for three reasons:

- Preventing a loss if the market is driven lower.
- Looking for buying opportunities.
- Considering taking a profit in a market rally.

Since the specific direction of the volatility is unpredictable, this situation is usually not ideal for short-term trading. Short-term traders, trying to outguess these situations, tend to get "whipsawed" by the highly volatile markets. Although taking advantage of options expirations can be at least part of a longer term strategy, the investor must be careful.

Chapter 39

Buy on Monday—Sell on Friday

Publisher Yale Hirsch has devoted more than 20 years to the study of various historical stock market trends. His book and annual almanac have been quite popular with traders and investors.[1] Buying stock on Monday and selling on Friday has long been established as a market strategy. According to Hirsch's study, it looks something like the chart on the next page.

Although these are indeed interesting statistics, two points should always be kept in mind:

- Former performance does not predict future happenings.
- If 43 percent of Mondays closed lower than the previous Friday, it means that 57 percent closed higher or unchanged. That is also a significant number.

Calendar trading systems do have many fascinating statistics. Some go back 30, 40 or more than 50 years. Although they have a certain amount of validity in terms of the odds of an occurrence, they are often difficult to rely on when making actual trades buying and selling stocks. Some investors also

---

1   *Stock Traders Almanac.*

Market Performance Each Day of the Week
(June 1952–June 1985)

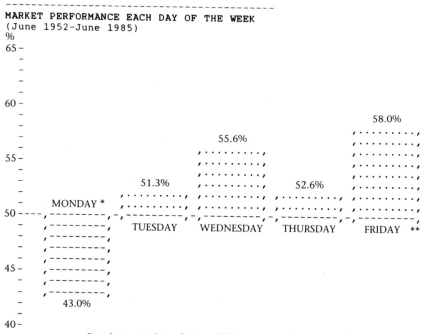

MARKET PERFORMANCE EACH DAY OF THE WEEK
(June 1952-June 1985)
%

Based on number of times S&P composite index closed higher than previous day.

*   On Monday holidays, the following Tuesday is included in the Monday figure.

**   On Friday holidays, the preceding Thursday is included in the Friday figure.

(Source: *Don't Sell Stocks On Monday*, by Yale Hirsch, published by Penguin Books, 1987, page 17.)

believe there are preferable times of the day to buy and sell stocks. Some believe that certain days of the month are better than other days or that one time of the year is better than another time.

This is the stuff of the statistician. That same number cruncher who says a person can be standing on a block of ice with one foot, have the other foot in a blazing fire and yet the person's overall temperature is, statistically speaking, comfortable. As with other systems, heavily dependent on numbers, there are important additional concepts.

Tendency and Possibility

Even though statistics can show certain tendencies and patterns, the market does not generally move because of these patterns. Rather, the patterns are created by other economic events that tend to occur at similar times. If these economic events change, the pattern will also be likely to change. A perfect example will probably be shown by the IRA effect in the month of April. Now that IRA new money has been significantly reduced, will the first half of April cease to be one of the strongest gain periods?

Another consideration is the length of time covered by the statistics. If the statistician goes back 20 or 30 years it is possible that the most significant data occurred in an isolated time period and skewed all of the figures. It could be more interesting to compare the data to three year or five year statistics as a further control. This is not meant to be critical of any statistician or any publication such as the one by Mr. Hirsch. Rather it is a caution all investors should have in following systems and indicators that are based on statistics.

Calendar statistics are interesting and worth being aware of when planning strategy. It might not be possible to count on a Santa Claus rally to appear just before Christmas, but it is worthwhile to be aware of the possibility and take advantage of the situation.

Chapter 40
Never Get Married to the Stock

Investors will often get married to just a few types of stock. It might be the stock of a company they once were employed by or it might be the stock of a company which has a new miracle product; miracles such as: "this company has a product that will automatically cool a can of soda pop."

This is often the kind of stock people end up getting married to, much to their total frustration. They are willing to stay with it through thick and thin, sickness and in health, etc.

The ideas are exciting, one even might say irresistible. Often the management has a well-known name in some capacity other than business management. A heart surgeon can be the best specialist in the country but makes a terrible corporate president.

A lot of money goes into these start-up companies, and when the stock is issued it might run up for a short while. Before long, the stock has dropped back to the original price and below. Many times the stock languishes for several years with very little movement. The stock doesn't perform well for many reasons, some of which are listed here.

No Earnings: The company is often new and barely getting by on a small amount of money left over from paying off the venture capital group who brought the stock public.

Management: The worlds greatest physician might not be a good CEO, a former astronaut or famous athlete could have trouble as a company president. Upper management should be from a similar business or at least have a solid background in business. Often times high-profile professionals are too accustomed to having many details done for them without having to fight for results. In a new company, it is usually a battle for results from the top to the bottom of the organization.

Product: The product might be ahead of its time and may not have a realistic market or the product can be stuck in a development stage, forever. In some cases there might not even be any intent to actually bring the current finished product to market. The public sale of stock could be solely for the purpose of returning capital to the venture capitalist or the company hopes to pick up a viable product along the way.

Financing: The company might not be able to obtain the necessary financing to successfully manufacture the product and supply it in sufficient quantities.

Lawsuits: Start up companies often have lawsuits from unhappy employees or money lenders. Another source of lawsuits is patent infringements. Sometimes these lawsuits get nasty and time consuming. This can tie up assets and hamper the abilities of management to keep the company going.

These are often the kinds of stocks people buy and never want to let go. The price drops and the investors hang on, hoping they might get lucky. Sometimes luck will prevail and the company eventually recovers, but this can take several years. The gain on the investment might not be worth the wait. It is usually better to take the loss and move on.

Investor's sometimes get married to stocks of larger, well-established companies as well. Usually this is a case when the person has been an employee of the company. They buy the stock as it is dropping in price and hang onto the stock because they know how "well run" the company has been in the past. It could have been well run when they worked for the company, but times have changed and often this is why the stock is having a difficult time. The company is no longer well run or it has been unable to adapt to changes in business.

The unfortunate decline of Western Union was to the financial disappointment of many former employees, who bought the stock as the price continued downward. Actually, an individual might even know more about the competition than they do about the future of a company that has employed them. In fact, many times it could be better to invest in the stock of a competitor. The investor would be less forgiving during the hard times.

Chapter 41

Diversification Is the Key to Portfolio Management

If the title to this chapter were totally correct, nearly any diversified mutual fund of stocks would be the perfect investment, and that is just not the case.

Diversification of investments has been bandied about like some child's favorite rag doll. Actually, it only has a few useful functions and doesn't even begin to offer the kind of protection many people think it does.

Diversification is the placing of financial assets into significantly different investments for the purpose of increasing the chances of larger profits, improving a degree of safety and simplifying the analysis/selection process.

"Significantly different investments" does not mean buying the stock of three different computer companies. Seagate Technology, Digital Equipment and Apple Computer are fine companies, but investing in these stocks alone would not necessarily be good diversification. If one invests in a computer company, a food company, and a department store company the mix is certainly diversified in significantly different areas. They are still somewhat bound by general economic conditions, but the diversification is definite.

Chances for larger profits are enhanced by having more shots at the profit target. It is often difficult to know where the next rapid economic growth will appear. Investing in the stocks of companies in different areas of the economic structure will increase the chances of participating in a surge when it occurs.

Safety is improved by not putting all the investment money in the stock of one company or industry ("Don't put all of your eggs in one basket"). If one company falls on hard economic times and the price drops, the impact is not as great if the investor also has other stocks that are continuing to do well. This is, however, a narrow safety focus. Overall market safety is little improved since all of the stocks are likely to decline in price as the stock market drops.

For many years people have been led to assume that market safety is improved by diversification, whether in individual stock portfolios or in mutual funds. In fact, the chances of improving profits with diversification are more highly probable than the possibilities of providing greater market safety.

If an investor owns the stocks of ten different companies and the market declines severely, all ten will likely drop in price. If the market is stable, this diversification will provide ten chances for one great stock and more chances for other good stocks.

Analysis and selection can be easier with diversification. Since the odds of choosing "a good stock" have been improved, by the number of different investments, the same quantity of intense analysis necessary for choosing just one stock has diminished.

It is rather difficult to predict the highest growth industry over the next ten years and even more difficult to choose the one company which will be the leader. On the other hand choosing three or four potentially high growth industries and five or six stocks which could be leaders is not as difficult. This is not to say that the investor should not be careful, but rather that the selection should be less difficult since the chances for success are significantly increased.

In the past few years "financial planning" and "asset allocation" have become investment buzz words. They can help provide the investor with an overall investment plan and are worth consideration. However, it is important to remember that one of the goals of the brokerage firm is to have control of most or all of the investor's assets. In many cases financial planning makes an investor jump through a number of analysis hoops only to figure out which mutual funds will receive the investment. The conclusion is predetermined.

Most people work long and hard for their money. If a decision has been made to invest that money in the stock market for a higher return, a person should also work hard at investing that money wisely. The investor should take the time to learn about financial planning and undertake to do the actual analysis. It is not all that difficult. A good financial planning book can help the investor understand the basics. If the investor does not want to take the time to learn these basics it is probably best to stay with Money Market investments, Certificates of Deposit (CDs) and U.S. Treasury bonds.

This brings up two other forms of diversification, which do not necessarily maximize the return on investment, but do protect the principal.

The simple form of diversification is buying U.S. Treasury bonds and using all or part of the interest for other investments, such as buying stocks. In this approach the principal (original investment dollars) is never at any significant, direct risk as long as the bonds are held to their maturity date.

Another form of easy diversification is to take half of the investment money and buy zero coupon U.S. Treasury bonds with a maturity long enough for the actual dollar value to double. The other half of the funds can then be invested in other securities with higher risk. Again, the principal is protected if those bonds are held to maturity.

In both of these situations there are only two areas of risk. The money is essentially locked in at a set interest rate. If interest rates rise, the investor will not be able to easily take advantage of these higher rates. The second area of risk is with the portion of money invested in other securities. If the funds invested in stocks are totally lost it would be as if the money were not invested. Although this loss can happen, it is not likely that carefully selected stock investments would all go to zero. This strategy can be effective for limiting risk in the stock market.

Diversification is important in an investment strategy. It can help to increase the profits, provide some safety and make the analysis somewhat simpler. The investor should keep in mind that risk is somewhat controlled though not entirely eliminated.

Chapter 42

Partial Liquidation Might Be the Answer

"Reduce your line down to a sleeping point!"
Robert Rhea.

Uncertainty often causes the greatest frustrations in life. Uncertainty in the stock market should lead the investor to some sort of strategy. Some people have the patience to wait for an anticipated development and others simply cannot be comfortable waiting.

Although most investors will usually sell an entire stock position at once, this total action is not required. A block of a thousand shares can certainly be sold in lots of five hundred, one hundred shares or even less. This will cause the commission rates to be higher, but in some situations this strategy can be worth the additional cost.

Selling part of a stock position can be a good strategy, especially in a corporate takeover situation. Until the deal is done and paid for it can still fall through. The stockholder with a substantial quantity of shares should seriously consider selling at least some of the position. This is not the time to become over-concerned with a few dollars or even a few hundred dollars in commission. If the takeover stock has doubled in value and the buyout fails, the stock will go back to its former level or lower. This can represent thousands of dollars in lost profits.

If an investor is concerned that the stock market has stalled and is acting in an unpredictable manner, it can be prudent to sell part of the portfolio rather than entirely liquidating all of the positions. Selling part of a position can protect some of the profits and hopefully allow the investor to sleep better.

Chapter 43

Act Quickly,
Study at Leisure

A question from a customer to a broker might go like this:

> ". . . that's right, I want to buy 500 shares of XYZ at
> the market. By the way, how are Apple Computer
> and IBM doing?"

This is the *wrong time* to check on other information. When the broker reads back the order (an action which every investor should insist upon) let that order be placed immediately. This is not the time to be interested in other information of any kind. The market price on a stock is only good until the next trade. While the investor is placing an order it is possible for hundreds or even thousands of others to be placing similar orders. The market for XYZ could change considerably in just a few minutes. If other information is desired, call back later.

The same concept can be extended to the action decision. Once a course of action has been decided upon it should be acted on at the earliest opportunity. Waiting a day or even a few hours can change the situation to something entirely different.

Study and planning strategy do not mix together well with implementation. They should be done as altogether separate activities. This will help prevent taking actions based on partial information and will make the analysis more effective when planning strategy.

Chapter 44

Records Can Make Money

Recordkeeping can be an important investment. Records of trades, confirmation slips and monthly statements can provide information that will actually be worth extra dollars. At tax time nothing can be more frustrating than trying to find records of transactions for checking dividends and capital gains.

One of the biggest mistakes made by investors is having the stock certificate delivered and placed in a safe deposit box with no other records. Years later the investor will wonder what the cost of the stock was at the time it was purchased.

The "confirmation" notice of the buy should be clipped to the stock certificate when it is stored. This will save endless headaches figuring capital gains when the stock is sold.

The IRS has an easy method of figuring the cost basis when the owner is unable to do so. The entire proceeds from the sale are considered a capital gain and taxes are paid on the entire amount, rather than just on the profits.

Save open order notices (good till cancelled) and match them to open order cancellation notices when they arrive. Whenever a limit order to buy or sell stock is placed on one of the stock exchanges, an open order notice is generated (many over-the-counter securities do not generate this notice). This informs the customer as to the details of the order. Check these notices carefully for accuracy, and keep the notice where it is easily accessible. This will help prevent placing the same order twice.

It can be irritating to sell the same stock twice and have to pay for the repurchase. When a buy or sell is executed the open order notice should be placed with the confirmation of the trade. These should be clipped to the certificate if it is shipped or filed in chronological order if the certificates are held at the brokerage firm. These notices can be more important than old cancelled checks and they should be kept in a safe place for a reasonable length of time (many investors keep them for the same length of time as tax records).

Monthly statements are also important records and should be kept for a reasonable length of time. Twelve statements a year is not a lot of paper. They can be helpful in tracking down possible errors or figuring out the details of transactions. Eventually stock certificates will be done away with and all securities will be held in book entry format only. This will make transaction papers and statements even more important records to keep.

The 1099 statement at the end of the year is the statement which goes to the IRS. That alone says how important the statement is and how long it should be kept in a safe place.

Stock certificates which are sent out to the buyer are also very important documents. They are similar to titles or even deeds. They can be replaced if lost or stolen, but this can be costly and time consuming. Significant losses can occur while the owner is waiting for the new certificates. Time is lost while a stop is placed on the old certificates and records are searched to ascertain whether or not the certificates have in fact been sold.

If dividends are being reinvested, see if the company will hold the certificates in account and have them issued in lots of 100 shares or more. This will prevent ending up with several hundred certificates, each worth two or three shares.

An organized system for keeping track of transaction records and certificates can save the investor time and money. The cost of having an accountant or lawyer sort out the details can be astronomical. Therefore recordkeeping is an important part of the investment process.

Chapter 45

In Most Cases Fraud Is Unpredictable

Anything can happen in the stock market. It is possible to research and select a stock for investment purposes that is about to double or triple in value and it is possible to select a stock which is just about to fold the tent and head for the cellar. The most unpredictable bad news to anticipate is the news of fraud within a particular company.

There has long been a kind of code of honor which says that all of the financial information that a company releases is composed of factual and accurate details. There are also securities laws that help to insure this accuracy. However, anytime integrity of information depends on codes of honor, somebody will always figure out a way to get around the system. Audits tend to only confirm the accuracy of the data presented. The auditors are limited in what they can uncover. If clever, fraudulent data is presented to them, there isn't much they can do. The investor, individual or institution has no way of knowing whether information available on any company is true or false. This is simply part of the risk of investing.

The expensive, national embarrassment of the crookedness in the Savings and Loan industry (S&L) shows that the problem of fraud is not limited to stock investing. In fact it is interesting that part of the problem with the S&L situation was the regulation of the investor protection, offered by the Federal Government Insurance. The penalties for fraudulent activities are not nearly as severe as the potential rewards. Even if the personal fortune of the perpetrator is reduced to zero, chances are a large amount of money is carefully hidden away where it either cannot be found or reached.

As the litigation develops and notices of stockholder settlements come out to the investor, one fact will become clear. Even though the settlement might look attractive, after the exorbitant legal fees are paid, the investor will be lucky to receive ten cents on the dollar for the settlement. These fraud situations are attractive plums for the lawyers. They take little risk, generate high volumes of paperwork and walk away with high fees for stating what was already known.

In most cases the investor is making a prudent move to sell at the first sign of fraudulent activity. The institutional investor will quickly sell off all or most of a position and the individual should do the same. In the majority of cases the news will not improve and will likely get worse. This is why it is important to quickly learn why a stock has a sudden severe drop in price. The investor must learn the content of the bad news and take the appropriate action.

In most cases it is impossible to see fraudulent information situations ahead of time. A personal visit to the company can be helpful but doesn't insure the integrity of the information. Companies tend to be good at putting on the "dog and pony show" for investors. Even the worst of companies can usually put up a good show for the right audience. The best defense for the individual is to be ready to sell a stock which has fraud as a problem.

Chapter 46

Use Margin
for Leverage Only

". . . and I've got 500 shares of stock worth about 80 dollars a share. I'd like to take out a margin loan so I can buy a new car. I figure twenty thousand will do it."

This statement or one like it is often heard in the broker's office. Someone has some stock which might have been sitting in a safety deposit box for many years. It could be nearly forgotten stock they bought some time ago or it might be stock from an estate. After reading or hearing about margin loans using stock as collateral, the old stock suddenly becomes an easy source of money.

The question a lot of brokers would like to ask next is, "When you get a margin call are you willing to sell the car to cover?"

Could it come to that? Yes, it could. This investor could end up without the stock and have to sell the car to cover the margin. Brokers and their firms do not like to see these problems develop because the customer loses and often ends up wrongly blaming the broker or the firm.

Being able to meet margin calls, is why many brokerage firms will require 40 percent margin maintenance (instead of the usual 25 or 30 percent) if the customer is margined on a small number of stocks. The debit (amount borrowed) remains constant whether the stock price rises or falls.

If an investor borrows 50 percent of the value of one stock and that stock drops a bit more than 10 percent in price, the investor will most likely receive a margin call to bring in funds as soon as possible. This could put the investor in a difficult financial situation. If the market and the stock are stable there might not ever be a problem, but the risk is always present in a margin situation.

The risk of margin loans, with securities as collateral, can be quite high. As was discussed earlier (see Chapter 34), the investor can end up losing all the securities and owing extra money. Therefore margin should be used with a great deal of care and understanding.

Margin loans should be used primarily to leverage an investment position. Although the cash is available and can be used for any purpose the investor desires, it is most prudent to use the funds to buy additional marginable securities. The reason for this is liquidity. If the securities decline in price, part of the position can be easily sold to cover the entire margin call or totally liquidated to cover the margin loan. Selling stock or other securities is generally easier than selling a car, a weekend cabin or the children's college education in order to meet a margin call.

As an investor becomes more familiar with margin loans, through study and experience, the use of margin loan funds can be expanded. But until the skills are developed it is better to be conservative and careful. Margin loans are best used to leverage a securities position.

Chapter 47
Avoid Overtrading

For some people, the trading of stocks, options or other securities can become an addiction, an addiction similar to a gambling addiction. It can be like a nickel or dime slot machine—win a few jackpots and keep putting the coins back in until they are gone. It is like the need to bet on one more horse to make up for the losses.

Similar to those with other gambling addictions, the trading addicted person is usually not making any money. At best they tend to break even, which only adds to the compulsive activity. The day is not complete unless they can make one or two stock or option trades.

Every brokerage firm has a few stories of a stock or option trader who became addicted to trading. The stories usually involve fairly large sums of money over a few years. Eventually, the trading addicted investor runs out of money or the brokerage firm's compliance department steps in and puts a halt to the activity. Compliance departments are often quite diligent in this regard, though it is difficult for them to closely watch every account.

One such story involves an investor who became addicted to trading index options on the Standard & Poor's 100 Index, often referred to as the OEX Index. During a three-year period, this investor traded an average of two and one half times per day for each trading day. He consistently lost an average of $10,000 per year for a total amount just over $30,000. This does not take into account the value of the hundreds of hours spent in research that went into the trading decisions.

The customer's biggest disappointment was not the money lost, but rather being forced to close the account due to not being able to maintain the 2000 dollar equity required for a margin account.

This investor did have a disciplined approach to investing. Sometimes the strategy was successful and other times it failed to produce anything but losses. The system was possibly too inflexible to deal with the daily changes in the stock market and it was not helped by a compulsive need to make a trade every day.

The main failing of this compulsion seemed to be the missed opportunities caused by closing out the option positions too soon. In several of the situations, the investor had the right idea but did not allow time for the strategy to do its work. If patience lasting only a couple of days had been used, the positions would have been profitable.

The news in April of 1990 had an example of another individual addicted to trading Standard & Poor's 100 options (the OEX Index). When successful, this person would make several million dollars in a single day. Eventually the system quit working as well and he began to lose on the trades. Finally the investor was forced to quit trading altogether. His personal fortune, as well as (allegedly) money of his friends and clients was gone. Losses approaching twenty million dollars were estimated. All of these losses were attributed to trading addiction. This malady had a detrimental effect on his fortune, his livelihood and his family life. It was nearly as destructive as the worst kind of drug addition.

Individuals addicted to trading are either losing money or about to begin losing money. Strategies that had been working for them will eventually work against them (part of the argument for flexibility in strategy). As the losses begin to mount, addicted individuals quit using strategy altogether and just keep on making trades, hoping for a turn in luck. They have neither the patience nor the flexibility to analyze the changes in the market or what they are doing wrong.

Overtrading can be difficult to control, especially with such things as the rise in popularity of trading stocks on a personal computer. This flexibility may encourage the investor to do more frequent trading. Carefully checking records can help the investor prevent overtrading. Taking the time to analyze the trades on the monthly statement can help the investor stay in control of the amount of trading. Other ideas to prevent overtrading are explored below.

Keeping Organized Records: Look carefully at the monthly statement and make a short note as to the reason for the trade. If the investor normally does a lot of trading in a month, these notes should be kept on the confirmation slips which arrive by mail.

The ideal situation could be to keep notes on strategy in a stock trading log. This way the notation is made at the time of the transaction, when the strategy is still fresh in the mind. The notation should briefly mention how the trade fit into the specific strategy and possibly the overall plan.

Looking For Profit In Transactions: If there are several unprofitable transactions, both buying and selling, it is time to reassess or redefine the strategy. In this situation, checking the timing of the trades can be helpful. Might the delay of a week or two have increased the profits? Perhaps the investor should check analysis of the current market strength.

Look For Patterns In Trading. Are trades occurring every day or every other day? Is there a pattern such as trading every three out of five days on a consistent basis? If a pattern is noticed, what is the cause? Finding a pattern might point out trading which is becoming an addiction.

How Much Contact With The Broker. Is this contact on a daily basis or is it several times a day, perhaps even hourly? This close contact with the market can easily lead the investor to overtrading the account. The individual can develop a kind of addiction to the market action. The information addiction can cause the person to overreact to minor moves in the market. The first overreaction leads to another and soon the account is in an overtraded tailspin.

This addiction to stock market information is quite common. Many clients are constantly calling for market updates and quotes. Although the constant need for market information does not always lead to trading addiction, it still does have that potential. One way to resist this need for information is to keep in mind that too much information can be as bad or worse than no information at all. It tends to become confusing. This is true, even for the experts.

Index Options Seem To Be More Addictive: That is more addictive than regular stock options. Perhaps because they can be so much more volatile in a hyperactive market. They are based on large numbers of companies (20, 30, 100, 500 different companies) and therefore move as the market tends to move. (An ordinary stock option, of course, is only based on the movement of the stock of just one company.) This larger company base seems to magnify the volatility of index options. The premiums can rise to much higher numbers, which is why they are attractive, or fall much more rapidly than regular stock options.

Overtrading and trading addiction can be detrimental to any investment strategy. It is extremely difficult to build profits when too many transactions are being whipsawed by short-term market swings. Flexible strategies, good records and the ability to pull away from unprofitable market activity will help to prevent overtrading.

Chapter 48

Buy When There Is Blood in the Streets

Every time the stock market takes a plunge this axiom is taken from the shelf and dusted off. It is the kind of saying many people believe makes a lot of sense. Actually, it can be disastrous as a strategy.

In 1929 and 1930, the stock market plummeted. The DJIA hit a high of 381 and a low of 198 in September of '29. In April of 1930, it ran back up to 294 and fell to another low of 158 in December. It kept this up until July of 1932 when the Industrials logged a low of 41.22. Those who waited until that summer of 1932 and then invested their money (assuming they had any left) did fairly well, if they chose the right stocks.

The problem was that a number of family fortunes were lost along the way as people believed they were buying stocks at bargain prices. Obviously, it could have been good to buy the right stocks when the market hit bottom in 1932, but the question remains, what are the right stocks? In the 1930s, many companies continued to weaken until they went out of business.

Economic setbacks are now called recessions and not depressions, but the effects can be similar. The economic structure of the nation is now based on global considerations. This helps to create a moderating buffer when the economy and the market slip. Severe stock market declines are now regarded by many as distinct buying opportunities and so far this has been true. But overall recessions or "rolling recessions," which go from industry to industry can still create tough economic times. It is always difficult to know how severe a market drop will be in the final analysis. Individual stocks can be an even larger problem.

If a stock takes a sudden and severe decline that is not market driven, the company is having serious problems from which it might never recover. At the very least, the company will have to resolve the fundamental problems that caused the price decline. If a stock buyer chooses such a stock for investment, it is important to either be well acquainted with the industry segment involved and the company's ability to recover or to buy the stock on total speculation with the intention of holding the stock until it recovers. At times the prices of these stocks will fall quite low. Some may drop below a dollar a share.

Some of these speculative stock buyers believe that it is easier for a two dollar stock to double in price than it is for a twenty dollar stock to double. In-depth study will find that the opposite is true in the majority of cases. In fact, it is often the 25 dollar or even 45 dollar stock that will quickly double in price. The reason for this is that an increase in price is not based totally on the price itself, but rather on value based on price, earnings and earnings anticipation.

If an investor is tempted to "buy when there is blood in the streets," first make certain that the patient is well on the road to recovery.

Chapter 49

Look for Divergence in Trends

The stock market almost never has a "normal" day. Upon fine analysis, each day is unique with its own special pattern of changes. One day technology stocks will be hot and oil stocks will be out of favor. The next day it might be the oil stocks that are the main focus. One day the Dow Jones Industrials will be up 20 points and the outlook for business development appears in sight. The following day the market could correct 15 points and inflation is seen as a real threat.

As J. Pierpont Morgan so succinctly put it, the market will indeed "fluctuate," it will be up unless it drops and it will drop unless it rallies. What the market does on a day-to-day basis is important in the way it contributes to or detracts from the current trend. These daily moves of the market are significant for short-term analysis.

The current trend of the market is important. The longer term (primary trend) shows the overall direction of the market. The shorter term (secondary trend) shows a reaction or move opposite to the primary trend. The day-to-day movements (tertiary trend) are important mainly in the way they contribute to the formation of the other trends. The market moves in trend patterns and individual stocks move in trend patterns.

The direction of the trends is important for the individual investor. Understanding the trend will help time the buying and selling of stock, whether for the short-term trade or the long-term hold. The one point that all analysts seem to agree upon is that the prices of stocks appear to move in groups. Dow Average stocks move as a group, Standard & Poor's 500 stocks move as a group, industries move as a group and the stocks of similar companies move as a group.

This tendency of stocks moving as a group is what makes up a trend. Divergences are changes in the trend that signal possible turning points. Even though it is often difficult to know whether the change will be a turn in the primary direction or merely a secondary reaction, the investor who is aware of the divergences in trends and other indicators can use them to an advantage. First the signal, then the reaction, then the turn in direction. This sequence can be illustrated by the events surrounding the 1987 crash:

- the new all-time high for the Dow Industrial was reached in August,
- then the signal, a rise in interest rates (the Federal Discount Rate was raised),
- next was the reaction (the Dow Industrials had drifted 200 points lower by October 19),
- finally came the turn in the trend as the Dow Industrials fell more than 500 points. Even though a similar pattern accompanies all market turns, it is seldom identical.

Signals can be confusing; a market trend can ignore what is supposed to happen and continue on its merry way. It can do this because it is a market of individuals buying and selling stock. Though institutionally dominated and locked into computer programs, the market is still influenced by individuals making judgment calls.

Many times everyone involved is waiting for someone else to make a move. Groups form, believing the market might fall. Still other groups form and take action which will prove the first group wrong. As the struggle ensues, buying or selling groups will gather and lose supporters until finally a majority of buyers or sellers emerges.

The participants in this market struggle will make use of news and information to support their belief with an action of either buying or selling stock.

All the individual investor has to do is look for signals of a brewing struggle. These signals will first appear in divergences in trends. (See page 204.)

As we look at the closing levels of the three Dow Averages from December 1989 through early April of 1990, we see some interesting divergences in trends.

Although the Transportation Average confirmed the January 2 rally in the Industrials, it was a weak confirmation. The Transports were significantly below an earlier high, which was attained in the first part of December. Both averages then continued to drop until the end of January when they appeared to hit bottom and rally.

They rallied for the next couple of weeks and then dropped once again to a similar bottom. Since this second drop did not significantly fall below the first bottom it was a bullish signal. This is often referred to as a "double bottom," and establishes a strong support level for the market trends. A strong support level says that it will be difficult for the averages to fall below this level. Difficult but not impossible. In fact, if the average does fall significantly below this level, it will most likely fall considerably lower until another area of support is reached or established.

Late March and early April show another support area being etablished with a definite double bottom in the Industrials and a less clear support level in the Transportation Average.

The steady decline in the Utility Average is a concern. This decline is a reflection of an increase in interest rates. The stock market does not like rising interest rates because they have a negative impact on earnings. The divergence of the Utility Average is a caution sign, though not necessarily a clear sign of retreat. Interest rates can also be volatile and suddenly drop, improving the picture.

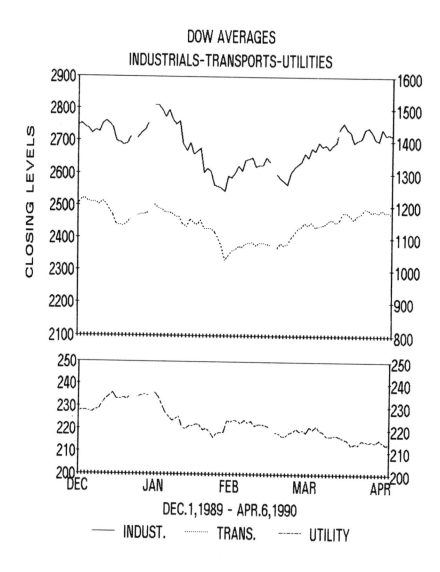

DOW AVERAGES
INDUSTRIALS-TRANSPORTS-UTILITIES

DEC.1,1989 - APR.6,1990

—— INDUST.   ········· TRANS.   ----- UTILITY

Are the trends of the Dow Averages following a similar track, or has one trend line begun moving in a different direction? One can also compare the current Dow Averages to broader indexes, such as the S&P 500, or less volatile trend lines, such as a 200 day moving average. All of these trend lines should be essentially in the same direction. Divergence of trends can provide an early warning signal to a turn in the stock market.

Chapter 50
Invest In What You Know Best

Diversification is always advisable in an investment protfolio, but it also makes sense to invest in the industry segment or company related to the investor's personal work experience background.

If an investor works in the auto industry it is logical to do some investing in automobile stocks. The pharmacist should have some special insight into the potential growth in pharmaceutical companies and the electrical engineer could do well investing in the stock of high-tech companies.

Even though this makes sense, it is not always the case. Many investors insist on investing in companies or industries with which they have no familiarity. Doctors often invest in Aerospace stocks, Aerospace engineers invest in drug companies and drug company employees invest in high-tech computer companies.

The problem with this strategy is the investor's vulnerability to public relations. Because the investors are not familar with what is real and what is so much window dressing, it is more difficult for them to discern which information is significant.

These same individuals often have a great deal of knowledge about the workings of their own industry. They might have ten or twenty years practical experience that can be used as a basis for analysis. This experience can give them advantages not available to even the highest level analyst. Most good analysts would love the opportunity to work for 30 days in the companies they follow and do this work on an incognito basis. The knowledge gained would be priceless. However, analysts do not have the time for such an activity, much less the opportunity.

The indiviudual already has the work experience, so why not take advantage of the background? If the conclusions result in better investments, consider it a work-related bonus for making use of job-related knowledge.

This is not to say that an investor should invest only in the company which employs them, but rather to choose stocks in the same industry. In many cases, the investor will be able to look at financial or new product information and quickly perceive what is real and what is artificial.

It might be good to invest in the stock of a competitor; the advantages to this are:

- No emotional involvement with the stock.
- Early observation of new developments.
- Easily follow financial growth.
- Observe the occurrence of problems.

Investing in the stock of companies with which one has practical, working knowledge will not guarantee success, but it can help to make the analysis more meaningful and improve the chances of success. It can have the additional advantage of keeping an eye on the developments of the competition, which might help the investor with his regular employment.

GLOSSARY

ACQUISITION: When one company buys all or enough of the stock of another company to take over control of its operations. Takeovers can be clean or messy. Clean takeovers are either a total cash offer for the shares outstanding or a one-for-one stock exchange issued by the company implementing the acquisition. They generally have a positive effect on the price of the stock being acquired. Messy takeovers are a combination of stock, preferred stock or other securities and cash. They frequently have a negative effect on the price of the stock being acquired.

ARBITRAGE: A financial strategy that takes advantage of price differences. In the earlier days of slower communication, this was accomplished when the same stock would be trading at different prices on different exchanges. This arbitrage situation has been virtually eliminated with the advent of computers and increased speed of communication. Arbitrage trading now refers to trading stocks in highly volatile situations, with rapid and severe price fluctuations, or trading on the price differences between stocks and the stock index options and futures.

ASK: Also called the "offer," it is the lowest price a specialist on a stock exchange or trader on a trading desk (with OTC stocks) will charge for a stock being sold to an investor.

ASSIGNMENT: The notice to an option writer (seller) that an option holder (buyer) has exercised the option to purchase or sell and the option writer must deliver and fill the terms of the option contracts.

BETA: A measure of the volatility of a stock's price in comparison to the market. 1.0 Beta is essentially equal to the market. Less than 1.0 is less volatile than the market, and more than 1.0 is a greater volatility than the market. Sudden price fluctuations can distort the Beta, making it temporarily unreliable.

BID: The sell side of the stock quote. It is the highest price a specialist on the exchange or trading desk (with OTC stocks) will pay for a stock being sold by an investor.

BLOCK: A significantly large number of shares of stock or other securities. 10,000 shares or more is considered a block, but as few as 2000 shares will often receive block trading treatment and be handled by a brokerage firm's block trading desk.

BEAR MARKET: A steadily falling stock market.

BULL MARKET: A steadily rising stock market.

COMMISSION: A fee charged by a brokerage firm for purchasing or selling securities for its customers.

COMMON STOCK: Securities that represent shares of ownership of a corporation. Stock may be held privately, by one or more individuals; closely held, by the corporation and employees; or publicly traded, whether over the counter (through market makers) or traded on stock exchanges, such as the New York Stock Exchange and the American Stock Exchange.

COVERING: Purchasing a security that had been previously sold short. This purchase will close the position.

CURRENT YIELD: The percent paid out from a dividend on a stock or interest payment on a bond, stated in terms of the current market price of the security.

DAY ORDER: An order to buy or sell a security which will be cancelled at the end of the same trading day if it cannot be executed.

DEBIT BALANCE: The outstanding amount of a margin loan.

DISCOUNT: To adjust for or take into account; such as the stock market had already discounted the bad earnings for the third quarter and was relatively not affected by the news.

DISCOUNT RATE: The interest rate charged by the Federal Reserve Bank on cash loans to member banks.

DIVERSIFICATION: Investing in the stocks or other securities of significantly different companies and/or industries.

DIVIDEND: A payment made to current shareholders who meet the time ownership requirements. It is usually paid quarterly, most often in cash and pro-rated on a per share basis. Special dividends can be declared at any time and dividends can be in the form of additional shares of stock.

DIVIDEND YIELD: The amount of the cash dividend of a share of stock divided by the current market price or the price paid for a previously purchased stock. This figure represents the interest rate percent the investor will receive from the dividend alone.

EARNINGS PER SHARE: The available earnings of a company divided by the total number of outstanding shares of common stock.

EQUITY: Equity always refers to ownership. It is usually used as a synonym for common stock of a publicly traded corporation.

EX-DIVIDEND: "EX" means "without." A buyer of stock on or after the EX-dividend day will purchase the stock without getting the dividend. A seller of stock on or after the EX date will not sell the dividend with the stock. Any sale before an EX date will not entitle the investor to the dividend.

ISSUE: Any securities sold by a company, whether new or existing. The sale of a new additional security.

LEADING INDICATORS: A list of economic indicators (the leading 12) believed to help forecast the direction of the overall economy.

LIQUIDATION: The conversion of securities, such as stock or other properties, to cash.

LONDON INTERBANK OFFERED RATE (LIBOR): Effectively, the British equivalent to the PRIME RATE in the United States.

MANIPULATION: The illegal buying or selling of a security or securities for the purpose of creating a misleading appearance of active trading, whether buying or selling.

MARGIN: Borrowing money using securities as collateral.

MARGIN REQUIREMENT: Specifies the quantity of cash or equity requirements that must be on deposit with a brokerage firm or bank. Margin is determined by the Board of Governors of the Federal Reserve Board. Individual brokerage firms are allowed to maintain margin requirements that are stricter than those of the Federal Reserve Board.

MARKET ORDER: An order to buy or sell a stock or other security at "the best available price."

THE NATIONAL ASSOCIATION OF SECURITIES DEALERS, INC. (NASD): An association of brokers and dealers which sets self-regulatory rules and regulations applying to brokerage firms and their employees or representatives.

NATIONAL ASSOCIATION OF SECURITIES DEALERS AUTOMATED QUOTATIONS (NASDAQ): An automated information system that provides brokers, dealers and others with price quotations on securities traded over the counter.

ODD LOT: An amount of stock less than the 100 share "round lot."

OFFER: The price at which an investor can buy a security.

OPEN ORDER: A "good till cancelled" order.

PRICE-EARNINGS RATIO: The price of a share of stock divided by the earnings per share for a twelve-month period.

PRIMARY MARKET: The market for new issues of securities.

PRIME RATE: The interest rate charged by commercial banks to their best customers.

QUOTE: The statement of the highest bid and the lowest offer to buy and sell securities.

RALLY: A sudden, significant upward movement in the price of an individual stock or in the market as a whole.

REGULATION T: The federal regulation determining the amount of credit that may be advanced by brokers and dealers to customers for the purchase of securities.

ROUND LOT: A unit of trading or multiple units of trading. On the New York Stock Exchange, a round lot for common stocks is usually 100 shares. There can be exceptions to higher priced securities and other special situations.

THE SECURITIES AND EXCHANGE COMMISSION (SEC): A U.S. Government agency set up by Congress to regulate and police the securities industry.

SETTLEMENT: The day on which securities purchases or sales are settled by the delivery of cash or securities.

SPLIT ORDER: An order that is filled in smaller blocks over a period of time. If the order is unable to be filled on one particular day and is carried over to the next day or beyond, additional commission charges may result.

TRANSFER AGENT: The record keeper (often a bank) for the issuance of certificates to new shareholders and the destruction of certificates that are being converted to "street name" or have been sold.

STOCK AHEAD: A term that explains why an order has not been filled, even though the price may have been reported on a particular order at the investor's limit. Other orders at the same limit were the "stock ahead."

TRADER: Anyone who buys and sells securities on a regular and frequent basis, whether a professional or amateur investor.

TRADES: Orders to buy and sell stocks.

UNLISTED SECURITY: A stock or other security that does not trade on a stock exchange (such as over-the-counter stocks).

UP TICK: A transaction in the buy or sell of a security which occurs at a price higher than the previous trade.

Suggested Readings

A Time to be Rich, by Dr. Lacy H. Hunt. Published by Rawson Associates, 1987.

Dr. Hunt's book contains some excellent comparisons of economic cycles, investing cycles and even life cycles. In planning investments, the understanding of economic cycles can be as important as understanding stock market cycles. Likewise, just as there are times when an individual can afford to take risks and has the assets to invest, there are times in the life cycle when risk should be avoided. Acknowledging and understanding these cycles can help an individual plan the most effective investment strategy for any given time.

How to Make Money in Stocks, by William J. O'Neil, the founder of *Investor's Daily*. Published by McGraw-Hill, Inc., 1988.

This is a book with practical analysis based on the structure of the informational data appearing in *Investor's Daily*. Mr. O'Neil has many practical ideas for the individual investor. His "C-A-N S-L-I-M method of analysis can help the individual learn a great deal about individual stocks and the movement of the stock market.

Margins & Market Integrity, by the Mid America Institute. Published by Probus Publishing Co., 1990.

This book represents a collection of the most valuable, authoritative and up-to-date research on the subject of margins, helping the reader cut through all the confusion and conflicting positions concerning margins. *Margins and Market Integrity* includes the following topics: margins—a review of the literature and evidence; understanding equivalence between stock and futures margins; margins and future contracts; margins and market integrity; margins setting for stock index futures and options; a review and evaluation of federal margins regulations; and margins and stock market volatility.

One Up On Wall Street, by Peter Lynch with John Rothchild. Published by Simon and Schuster, 1989.

Mr. Lynch is the well-known former portfolio manager of the mammoth Fidelity Magellan Fund, a mutual fund. With a down-to-earth approach, this book looks at many aspects of investing in stock and is particularly good in the discussion of stock selection.

Strategic Investment Timing in the 90s, by Dick Stoken. Published by Probus Publishing Co., 1990.

First published in 1984, *Strategic Investment Timing in the 90s,* has been completely revised and expanded to show how investors can use changes in the economic cycle to enhance profits in the stock, bond, metals and futures markets. Author Dick Stoken has studied investing for years and has devised a formula that has retroactively accounted for every major turn in the economy since 1920. Stoken shares with readers his hard-won knowledge: that the direction of the economy can be determined by following four simple, accessible and fundamental indicators (the Dow Jones Industrial Average, the rate of inflation, interest rates and the four-year presidential election cycle). Once the indicators have been identified and clearly analyzed, Stoken offers specific advice on how to adjust portfolios and investment choices based on what these indicators show.

Investment Periodicals

Informative Articles

AAII Journal, American Association of Individual Investors, 625 N. Michigan Avenue, Suite 1900, Chicago, IL 60611. (312) 280-0170.

Technical Analysis of Stocks and Commodities, Seattle, WA. 98146-0518. (800) 832-4642.

The Insider Transactions Report, Mark Les, P.O. Box 1145,1 Costa Mesa, CA 92628. (800) 333-2019.

The Personal Investor, Circulation Dept., 18818 Teller Ave., Suite 280, Irvine, CA 92715. (714) 851-2220

Charts

Trendline (a division of Standard & Poor's), 25 Broadway, New York, NY 10004. (212) 208-8792.
Various market analysis comments and charts on individual stocks.

The Value Line Investment Survey 711 Third Avenue, New York, NY (800) 633-2252
Contains long-term charts on the market and individual stocks as well as analyses of those stocks.

Daily Newspaper Financial Information

The Wall Street Journal, Editorial and publication headquarters, 200 Liberty St., New York, NY 10281. (Check local listings for regional phone number.)

Investor's Daily, 1941 Armacost Ave., Los Angeles, CA 90025. (213) 477-1453.

The New York Times, 229 West 43d Street, New York, NY 10036. Circulation information: (800) 631-2500.

Publishers will send subscription information and sample copies on request. Many also have shorter term "trial subscriptions."

About the Author

Michael D. Sheimo is an internationally recognized expert on the stock market, with books also published in India and Malaysia. He is the author of the critically acclaimed *Dow Theory Redux*, (Probus 1989) of which *The Wall Street Journal* reported "If you trade stocks . . . you should learn its [Dow Theory] fundamentals. It would be harder to find an easier way to do so than Michael Sheimo's book." Mr. Sheimo has more than twenty years of experience in business, education and the stock market. He was a stockbroker and Registered Options Principal for several years with both discount and full service brokerage firms. He currently works as a business consultant and investment advisor in Minneapolis, Minnesota.